WHAT HAPPENS NOW?

A Journey Through Unimaginable Loss

DAVE LUCK

RIVER
PUBLISHING

River Publishing & Media Ltd
Bradbourne Stables
East Malling
Kent ME19 6DZ
United Kingdom

info@river-publishing.co.uk

ISBN978-1-908393-73-9
Cover design by www.spiffingcovers.com
Printed by MBM Print SCS Ltd, Glasgow

Contents

Dedication

~

Benjie,
A bright light that shone all too briefly, but illuminated
many, many lives.
Our beautiful, precious boy.
We will always love you.

What Others Are Saying...

"As long as the unimaginable stays the unmentionable, then the question, 'What happens now?' will often be unanswerable. This book bravely and honestly faces the hard questions on each step of a very personal and painful journey. It doesn't give easy answers or formulas to follow, but something much better: hope."
Colin Piper, Executive Director World Evangelical Alliance Youth Commission

"This heart wrenchingly, honest and deeply stirring book should be read by everybody. It's the story of a journey that no parent wants to take and yet Dave conveys a deep sense of hope in the face of trauma that must be heard."
Carl Beech, Deputy CEO, The Message Trust

"Reading this book has stirred me deeply. *What Happens Now?* is the deeply moving account of one family's journey through loss, or more pointedly, 'unimaginable loss'. I have found it a real challenge to write these few words as they seem so inadequate an offering as a commendation for this book. All I can say is that this is an amazing story of a truly courageous family and their faithful and loving God. Be blessed as you read it."
Revd Canon Mick Woodhead, Team Rector, STC Sheffield

Introduction
~~~

The point at which our world fell apart was the time when we seemed to have it most together.

I'd got a new job the year before – the best paid and most promising I'd ever had. We'd got a better car and agreed to buy a bigger house. And the "we" was the most important bit. My family: my lovely wife, Louise, and my two delightful young boys, Joe and Ben. After a difficult childhood I'd got my own family and the chance to do family the way it should be done.

At the centre of all of this was faith – the Christian faith that had helped Louise and I get past our struggles and insecurities and build a positive life. I had recently taken on the shared leadership of a small independent church. Central to my understanding of my Christian faith was my belief in a God who could overcome anything. Who *could* and who *would*.

And now this...

Now I would see what my faith was made of when my world was turned upside down.

Chapter One
Beginnings

~~

"'For I know the plans I have for you,' declares the Lord,
'plans to prosper you and not to harm you, plans to give you
hope and a future.'"
(Jeremiah 29:11)

* * *

I was born on the 4th of April, 1974, in Bristol. Already, my life had been dramatically shaped. I was the second child of a married couple, but even as I was developing inside my mother, my world was experiencing a seismic shock. My Dad would be leaving soon after I arrived.

* * *

It's May 1987 and I'm away with my church youth group for the weekend. We are with another church from London and there's a speaker there called Andy. Andy is what is known in the Church as an evangelist – he just wants to tell people about Jesus. There may be plenty of other jobs to do in the Church, but that is his and he does it well, speaking articulately and with great passion. There is no pressure just invitation.

We've been going to church for a few years. A Vicar had started visiting our house each week to bring his friend for a flute lesson with my stepfather. My mum had a Christian background, but now discovered that Jesus wanted to know her personally.

So, I take the invitation and I ask Jesus to come into my life. I feel a euphoria I have never known before. I have met the living God.

* * *

It's millennium night and I am at St Thomas' Church, Crookes, Sheffield. I went to this church as a student and after University I did a training year here. Through that I joined a small church in the east of the city in a rough and ready place called Darnall, where I thought God had some work for me to do.

Tonight, I am back at St Thomas' for their millennium bash and I have my eye on someone. Louise and I have met a couple of times and made very little impression on each other, but then a few weeks back we got talking in the pub and a light went on for me. The problem is, I don't trust my instincts. I am far too quick to think someone is "the one". I have done it time and time again, driven by my insecurity and my need for a soul mate.

I have prayed today, determined not to let my imagination get ahead of me. But as it is, I see her in the crowded church and decide to go for it. We talk for most of the night. We get married on July 22nd.

* * *

It's June 4th 2010. I head into work as a council officer in Sheffield. Today there's a bit of pressure, as the team I manage has one of its regular meetings with the twelve city councillors we work with in the south east of the city.

My phone rings. Louise tells me that Ben (our youngest son, who is five) has been sick. Again.

Ben has been off colour for several weeks. He is constantly exhausted and every few days he is sick. Louise has taken him to the doctors and the children's hospital. We've been told it's a virus. The GP told the student doctor in her surgery, "There is clearly nothing wrong with this child." But Ben has been poorly for weeks and his eyesight is not right. We've taken him for an eye test. They couldn't see anything wrong.

Today, Louise takes Ben to the doctors again, where a practice nurse tells her to take him back to the children's hospital.

I go to my briefing, at which I am centre stage, bringing reports and introducing other speakers. I am agitated and check my phone constantly.

Louise rings. They have done a scan and found something. I later hear how the scanning room suddenly filled with doctors. Louise is distraught. Fortunately, I am only about half a mile away and my friend and colleague, Mick, gets me there in double-quick time.

I know where the children's hospital is, but am confused which entrance to take. The official entrance has no one at the desk. The signs make no sense. I run round to the A&E at the front of the hospital where Ben is in an assessment bay just around the corner.

Ben is in good spirits, but he tires easily and sleeps a lot. Louise tells me they have found a lump in his head. I go into the toilet and break down.

We spend as much time as we can chatting and playing with Ben and trying to act normal. Later the neurological team talk to us in a meeting room. They are approachable and compassionate, but they pull no punches. They want to reduce the swelling, which is causing the sickness. They will give hydrocortisone to replace the cortisol that Ben has stopped producing, which is why he is exhausted. They will operate soon; they do not hide the risks.

"What do I tell my son, Joe?" (who is seven), I ask.

"You need to tell him he could die," comes the response.

Chapter Two
The Life We Had

Life was busy and challenging, but life was good.

When we got married, Louise was working as a teacher and I was working for the church. In the few months between getting together and getting married, Louise, who had been teaching in Leeds, managed to get a job in Sheffield and we bought a house in Darnall.

A couple of years later our son, Joe, arrived and church formalised my position as Assistant Pastor. Two years on, Ben arrived. While life had its fair share of downs as well as ups, we had what we'd both craved: our own family, where we could be secure and not follow the pattern of our two sets of divorced parents.

It's not easy to describe the effects our parents' divorces had on us. Both were very different. I was a toddler and knew nothing about it at the time, but had to live with the consequences. My Dad has always been an active part of my life. We have a good relationship and have worked through all of the issues I have felt the need to bring up. I love my Dad and I have forgiven him, but we both know that the bottom line is that he did not bring me up.

My Mum and her second husband were very damaged people when they got together. Mum was left on her own with me and my sister, and my stepfather's first wife died suddenly, leaving him with two small boys. The combination was not one big happy family. I grew up in a cold, repressed environment where me, my sister, and our two stepbrothers learnt to plough our own furrows.

I grew up intense and insecure. I had few friends and no social life until I got involved with a citywide youth organisation at the age of fifteen. It was a shock to find people who seemed to not just like me, but also enjoyed my sense of humour!

When it came to girls I was desperate for companionship, but hopeless at friendship, so I just kept hoping for something to magically happen.

Louise was a teenager when her parents divorced. Whereas I had a quiet, polite, emotionally repressed split up to deal with, Louise had a loud, messy, traumatic one.

Both of us had left our home towns to study and very deliberately start again. I came to Sheffield because I liked the look of it and it was a long way from Bristol. Louise left St Helens to study at Nottingham before doing teacher training in Sheffield.

What we had in common with countless others was the fact that it's very hard not to feel a sense of rejection when your parents divorce. Whatever may be said, the consequence is *absence*. People try to fill that gap in different ways. I escaped into dreams, and one doomed scheme after another, to try and make things feel better.

This sense of rejection is married to the instability that comes from living with the effects of divorce. In some cases parents re-marry and provide a warm, secure environment, albeit with the complications of shared parenting across disconnected relationships. In many situations the pain from the separation is never far from the surface. The parent is wounded, the child suffers – often thrust into the role of counsellor.

The result is a lot of children like Louise and I, with a lot of hang ups. We'd both been unsuccessful at relationships in our own unique ways. I mostly had a trail of bemused no thank you's, while Louise had a bunch of messy, failed relationships.

Louise and I saw us getting together as the work of God. From that long chat on millennium night it became apparent in a matter of weeks that "this was it". It was so obvious that we just got on with it.

Our faith had been the context in which we both received a lot of emotional healing before we met. We were both used to churches that had an expectation that the Holy Spirit would show you things and bring breakthrough and release – so that the future wouldn't have to be shaped by the problems of the past.

Once we got married this process continued, with faith giving us the path to work out how to live together. Frankly, at the beginning, I just had no idea how to communicate. I'd never had much practice! Prayer was the tool for resolving arguments and learning how to avoid repeating mistakes over and over again.

We wanted two kids and were more than happy to have two boys. This was us learning how families should work and while we had difficulties, as every family does, we had a good time. Louise and I were determined to pour ourselves into the boys and they grew up with a life full of play and stories and trips out. Joe and Ben grew into a fine double act. Our house is full of their *Star Wars* and *Thunderbirds* memorabilia, and pictures of them peeking out of giant boxes transformed into pretend vehicles.

A few months after Ben was born we had a pregnancy scare. We didn't want three kids and we certainly didn't want three very young children. It was negative. As soon as Ben was nine months old I booked in for a vasectomy. Our position was clear: we love our children, we just don't want any more.

At the consultation for the vasectomy, the doctor asked what we would do if something happened to one of our children. I remember being confident that nothing would happen to either of them. This was partly faith and partly complacency. They were healthy, we were healthy, the people and children around us were healthy.

I remember Ben being a tougher toddler than Joe, but we were also having to deal with the hard work of having two kids. Whereas Joe was articulate from a very young age, Ben communicated by grunts until he was nearly two. He was a very determined child who made it clear what he wanted and expressed his displeasure if he didn't get it.

As Ben got older, the speech, of course, came and his sense of humour and intelligence began to shine out. One time we went to the Early Learning Centre to buy Joe a toy piano when Ben was very young and hardly speaking. Ben sat on the stool with the display model and started banging away, occasionally turning to the microphone and saying, "Oh yeah"!

Louise and I had a shared understanding that the boys would have all the love and attention we could give them. This meant lots of time at the park, swimming and trampolining lessons and an annual holiday that mostly revolved around ice cream and getting wet. Ben always loved swimming. Once, when he was very small, I took him for a swimming lesson. I sat him on the side and got in and he promptly flung himself in the water. Ben spent hours running around the water park of a local playground in his wet suit.

Ben also loved school. When he was young he would come with me when I took Joe to nursery. Ben always broke free of my hand, squirmed through the queue and got inside. I had to wait to sign Joe in and then go and find Ben. That's the sort of kid Ben was: bold, fearless; the opposite of a clingy, shy kid. This meant he couldn't wait for his chance to go to nursery and then reception. Ben was in a class full of big characters and still made quite an impression. He had no hesitation in telling his teacher (and, if need be, the Head) exactly what he thought. As well as this, Ben was emerging as a very bright boy. This was initially less obvious than with the super-articulate Joe. Ben picked up reading and, before he got ill, would read things off billboards and shops as we drove past. He also inherited my head for numbers.

In the spring of 2010, Ben started going to football training and he was delighted to get his first Sheffield United shirt. I used to take him along and laugh at his flailing limbs and enthusiasm. Looking back, we can understand now why he stopped for a rest at football and swimming, and why he wanted to go and play outside less. His energy levels were dropping, but in too subtle a way for us to recognise. He adapted and continued to manage everything. We thought he had a lazy streak, and he probably did, but there was something else going on.

A few years into my Assistant Pastor role, the Pastor suggested it would be wise for me to get some experience of doing a normal job and managing church roles alongside that. This was a shock at the time, but undoubtedly a good call. Initially, I found a 4-day-a-week project officer role in the council, with Louise doing a day's supply work. A year in, I got a secondment to a more senior role and when the service was reorganised I got a permanent manager's role. This meant that as 2010 arrived, we were in a position to get a better family car and exchange contracts to move to a bigger house, where the boys could have a bedroom each.

Whilst working for the council I continued to have a leadership role in the church. The church was small, with only 20-30 adults and their kids, but it had a big desire to make a difference in the local community. As a small church we struggled to get our message out into the community and also with people's suspicions of us as a church that wasn't part of a traditional denomination. Beyond that, we struggled to try and maintain a busy and active church programme with all the work that involves.

By 2009 it had been agreed that the Pastor would step down and, in addition to my job, I would take on church leadership with Brian, a fellow member of the leadership team. I was clear on the approach I felt we needed to take. We needed to ask what the church was there to do and see if all the activity we were doing was necessary. In terms of connecting with the community, we needed to think of simple, fun activities we could do alongside friends outside the church to try and make the church and our faith more real and relevant to them. I was under no illusions that growing a small church in a largely unchurched area would be easy, but I was confident that this was the right way to go about it.

My faith at that time was built on the understanding that there was one God and that in sending His son Jesus, He had come to essentially fix the world. This meant that, in my view, there was pretty much nothing that couldn't be overcome by operating as faithful Christians.

My experience as a Christian so far had borne this out. God had found me by placing a number of things directly in my path: the Vicar visiting my Mum, the evangelist leading the church weekend, the youth organisation that had brought on my faith as a teenager. Along the way I had plenty of other experiences of words from God, or His direct intervention, that I could point to. As an example, I once sat in the balcony of St Thomas' church as a young man, feeling full of woe. Behind me was a man from North Wales who had never been to the church before. He was visiting the church to bring along a friend of his from Sheffield, who he'd been talking to about God for some time. The man from Wales tapped me on the shoulder and passed over a scrap of paper with the Bible reference Revelation 3 verse 8.

The verse says:

"I know your deeds. See, I have placed an open door before you that no one can shut. I know that you have little strength, yet you have kept my word and have not denied my name."

This was a verse I'd never noticed before, but which spoke directly to me. The conclusion was simple: Almighty God was talking to me.

My belief was that I was special to God, though no more

so than anyone else. He had made us all and wanted us all to have a great life by knowing Him through the death of His son, Jesus.

The church where I had grown up in Bristol had known this sense of God's reality, but not in a way where it felt like a very present reality. The Vicar did not believe in the idea that God's Spirit was active to give Christians spiritual gifts and lead them into works of power, such as healing.

Over time I rejected his ideas. I believed God was real and wanted to demonstrate this reality. I believed in a God who spoke, who broke through barriers and actively provided. I believed God had led me to Sheffield and provided a wife, jobs and houses, as well as much else along the way.

I am a person who likes simplicity and clarity, and prefers linear thinking. I was persuaded by the idea of "dominion theology", which states that the death of Jesus has overcome the work of the devil and thus undone the fall of Adam and Eve. In this thinking, if the sin that started with Adam and Eve is dealt with, then so is the effect of that sin – so we can get back to the original dominion where Adam and Eve were told to rule the earth.

In a nutshell, this theology said that Jesus has died for the sin of the world, so you don't need to put up with the bad stuff in life that comes from living in a fallen world. At the heart of this was the idea of physical healing.

I believed that God could not only heal (as I had seen and heard some evidence of), but always wanted to heal because in Jesus He had overcome the source of sickness.

So when Ben became ill, my response was clear. Ben was going to be healed.

He had to be.

Chapter Three
The Illness

~~~

I had never worried about my children being ill. It's not something that had even occurred to me. Looking back, I'd never encountered sickness much. A child of a friend at swimming lessons had cancer and we prayed for him, but it never made me question anyone's mortality. Just a few weeks before Ben was diagnosed we had to take Joe to the hospital for an appointment about the grommets he'd had in his ears. I remember seeing kids with feeding tubes up their noses and thinking, "Thank goodness that's not my child." Within months it was.

When you encounter sickness it makes you aware of how much sickness there is around. It's a bit like buying a new car and suddenly noticing the same model everywhere. You become aware of how separated sick and disabled people can be by their illnesses and conditions; of how "normal" healthy people aren't anywhere near as normal as you thought.

Now we were in hospital with a very sick child. With a child who could die.

We were transferred to the High Dependency Unit. Joe was with friends who would look after him that night. Once upstairs on the ward I made some calls to family and work colleagues. It was impossible to get the words out without crying.

That night we stayed with Ben. We tried to sleep on reclining chairs. I don't remember how much we slept, but I can't imagine it was much. You may think we were in a state of frenzy, but the reality is you have to adapt very quickly – the abnormal becomes normal. We still had Ben to look after, though he was asleep much of the time.

On Saturday, I went home to get some clothes and went to see Joe, who our friend Faith was looking after. Joe had had a great time and wanted to carry on playing with his friends. I explained things as best I could. Joe was upset. He had a little cry and wanted to get back to playing.

On Sunday he came into hospital to see Ben. For the first, but not the last time, we found out that you can have fun and laughter amidst sickness and tragedy. The ward was light and spacious. There were play specialists on hand to do activities with sick children who could manage, and their brothers and sisters. In addition, one of the nurses, Chris, who we would be seeing a lot more of, had as much fun with the kids as possible. This mostly involved spinning them round on chairs with wheels.

We were told that Ben would be going down for surgery early that Monday. We'd asked people to pray and asked a bunch of people to come in and pray with Ben before he went down for surgery. I have no idea what we told Ben; I guess we tried to tell him what we could in a calm and low key way. The hospital, as throughout all of Ben's treatment, were completely supportive of our desire to pray. But we didn't want to be shouting and wailing, so people prayed, gently but firmly for blessing and success.

I went down with Ben to the operating theatre. We didn't know if he would ever wake up again. He took his favourite blanket and a teddy.

We had been told the operation would take most of the day and were advised by one of the surgeons to leave the hospital. He was well qualified to advise us, as his daughter had had major heart surgery at three months old. We left the hospital and walked into town. I saw someone from work and avoided them. I didn't want to have to explain anything. We went on to Meadowhall shopping centre, getting Ben a Ben 10 balloon and some food from McDonalds. Louise's mum was at our house where we returned to wait. She had flown over from her home in Spain. She stayed in Sheffield for the next year.

We had been warned that Ben may not make it and also that he may not be brought round the same day. We got the call that evening. All was well. We arrived to find Ben sat up, shouting at his nurse. He was demanding water, which he wasn't allowed yet. Apparently, as they brought him around he booted the anaesthetist in the stomach. They were all delighted. Ben was so well that he was moved out of Intensive Care after just half an hour and back to High Dependency. Over the coming days he recovered from the surgery. We were told it had gone really well. Not all of the growth could be removed, because of where it was located, but it had gone from a 5cm lump to a lining on some veins.

A few days later we knew Ben was doing better when he was offered food and demanded a burger. He was brought a hefty quarter pounder and demolished it rapidly.

As he recovered we were transferred down to M3 – the ward for cancer and blood disorders. M3 was painted hospital green and felt very institutional. Though it was good that Ben had his own room, we felt isolated after the warm, hurly burly of High Dependency. I hated being in a cancer ward and was resistant to the idea that Ben had cancer. We were told the growth could be tissue that has kept growing slowly since birth. It is not.

In a few days we were told that Ben did have cancer. Ben would need cancer treatment. Louise was devastated. I was convinced it would be okay. We knew that cancer treatment is often effective and advancing all the time. Beyond this, my faith told me Ben would be okay. God had not made him ill and it was God's will for him to be healed.

* * *

Ben recovered well from the surgery and was able to come home for a few days before his treatment began. I had prayed that Ben would be able to walk out of the hospital, not leave in a coffin, and he did walk out into the car, laden with the huge amounts of cards and presents he had been given.

We had been told that Ben had something called a PNET tumour. Its position at the front of the brain made it hard to treat and meant it had not been possible to remove it all. Its effect had been to stop the production of cortisol (the hormone that gives energy) and the pressure on Ben's optic nerves had affected his peripheral vision.

Ben was to have four courses of chemotherapy, each of which would involve several days in hospital until his immunity levels rose to a safe level. These would be spaced over a number of weeks and would then be followed by a series of doses of radiotherapy. After this it was expected he would have very unpleasant high-dose chemotherapy.

Ben also had to have a line fitted into his chest for the drugs to go straight into his bloodstream.

Before Ben underwent his first dose of chemotherapy we set up a Facebook page called "Pray for Ben Luck", which we used to update the many people supporting us in prayer throughout Ben's treatment. The first post was on June 21st 2010:

Ben is 5 and after several weeks of ill health was recently found to have a 5cm brain tumour. Three days later he had a seven hour operation to remove the tumour. The operation was very successful, but it was not possible to remove everything and a biopsy showed the tumour to be cancerous. Ben is due to start chemotherapy on June 28th if he is clear of an infection he currently has.

We have been overwhelmed by the prayer support we have received and believe this has resulted in major progress towards Ben's return to full health. We have set this page up for those who have been praying to provide prayer requests and updates.

Thank you so much for your prayers. We thank God for you and would appreciate your future prayer support to see the battle for Ben's health won. We do not believe prayer is a matter of getting God to take notice, but praying against the work of the devil in making Ben sick.

Jesus said, *"The thief comes only to steal and kill and destroy; I have come that you may have life and have it to the full"* (John 10:10).

Please pray:

- Giving thanks for Ben's life and the joy he brings to those who know him
- Giving thanks that the tumour was found in time, the operation was so successful, and he has recovered so well from it
- Praying that the treatment he will receive will completely eradicate the tumour
- Praying for God's protection on his body during the treatment, so that while the tumour is destroyed his body remains strong and well. Specifically pray that his

pituitary gland, which controls his hormones, will be fully functional

- Praying that Ben's sight would be fully restored, that he would regain full vision in his left eye and that his optic nerves would be fully restored

"For I know the plans I have for Ben,' declares the Lord, 'plans to prosper Ben and not to harm Ben, plans to give Ben hope and a future." (from Jeremiah 29:11)

Louise and I generally had a pattern of alternating spending nights at the hospital with Ben. When things were stable I went to work. The support I had from managers and colleagues at the council was outstanding throughout.

Louise spent the first day and night with Ben following his first dose of chemotherapy, which was administered intravenously over a number of hours. The chemotherapy made Ben sick overnight and gave him diarrhoea. I took Joe to school in the morning and, as was our routine, drove to the hospital with the intention of seeing Ben and then going on to work. Our routine was then that I would return after work and Louise would drive home to see Joe. Joe would be picked up from the school by Louise's mum and would come up to the hospital two or three times a week.

When I got to the hospital, Ben's consultant rushed past me into the ward. I went in and found Ben's bed surrounded by staff. He had just had a fit.

About an hour later he had another. Louise was frantic and asked if he was going to die. When he came round he had lost sensation in one side of his body. At this point I needed to go and move the car as it was in a two hour parking bay – the joys of a city centre hospital! I got another parking spot and walked back with my head in a mess. I thought about praying and initially wondered what the point was. It felt like we were losing Ben a piece at a time. I decided to pray anyway. I made a decision that whatever happened I was not going to quit.

When I got back, I was reassured that the loss of movement would be temporary. The drugs given to stabilise Ben meant that he slept for most of the day. I went downstairs with him for a CT scan. When it was over Ben came round and sat up. He opened his eyes and had a startled expression. I thought nothing more of it at the time and stayed with him that night.

The next morning he came round, back on the High Dependency Unit, and it became clear what the expression the day before had been about. Ben could no longer see anything. I went to work on autopilot. In truth, I just wanted to get away. I sat on the tram to work staring out of the window and thinking, "Ben will never see any of this again." I was supposed to go to a big staff meeting, but I couldn't face it. I tried to work in my office, but realised I couldn't cope when the phone rang and I couldn't face answering it. I went back to the hospital. There we had a meeting with Ben's consultant.

The consultant told us to expect the sight loss to be permanent. We now had a blind child. Worse, the scan had shown that the reason for this was that the tumour was growing rapidly and had done so in the three weeks since the operation. We were floored. I rang my boss, not knowing what to do with myself. He said, "I don't want to see you tomorrow." He knew he wouldn't see me the day after that, because we had the small matter of a house move to deal with.

The next day we started to come to terms with a blind Ben. At lunchtime I got Ben a snack box from the canteen. In it was a sandwich, drink, a pear and a Kit Kat. Ben ate his sandwich. I looked at Louise to see whether we should offer him the Kit Kat or, like good parents, give him the fruit first. Then an amazing thing happened. Ben reached out and picked up the Kit Kat. It became clear that Ben could see something, however badly. This gave us huge encouragement after the trauma of the previous two days. We knew that a big prayer movement was developing.

That first weekend I had sent a quick email to a dozen people when I went home to pick up clothes. One friend got his whole church to pray the next morning. Another local church divided the day of Ben's operation into twenty-minute time slots, so that someone was praying all day. I recall a text from another friend: "500 people just prayed".

Whatever people's views on God, faith and prayer, no one could deny the phenomenal response we had from the church in the city. Our small church organised bringing a hot meal to the hospital every night through rush hour traffic. The children's hospital was world class in most respects, but not in its food. The reason we were able to move house in the midst of all of this was because Louise's mum, supported by friends from church, packed up our whole house. The people whose house we were buying allowed our friends to go in before we moved to paint the kids' rooms. On the day of the move we had about twenty people descend to help us empty one house and then fill another. Friends then went to Ikea for us and put up all the flat pack furniture.

We were able to bring Ben to his new home for a few days in between doses. Despite the setback with his vision, we still had hope.

* * *

One night Ben was sat on his bed at home when he asked us who the person in white on the end of his bed had been. None of us had been wearing white. We could only conclude it was an angel.

Throughout Ben's illness our faith sustained us and gave us hope. We had a simple faith that God was real and powerful enough to defeat Ben's sickness. When set against a God we believed had made the whole universe and loved it enough to send His Son to die to for it, we felt the cancer had to submit and leave.

The means for this is what Christians sometimes call spiritual warfare – essentially prayer. Our understanding was that Jesus had overcome the power of the devil who had made Ben ill. By faith we sought to call that victory into being where we were.

I have always known that to some people all of this sounds utterly ridiculous. Calling out to an invisible man in the sky does sounds pretty mad on face value. But then to me the idea that the whole universe is a random, purposeless fluke, which just happens to lead to and sustain intelligent life is a lot crazier. Louise and I had both experienced the reality of God in our lives and from the start our response was to get people praying.

As much as it may irk the likes of Richard Dawkins, most people do believe in God in some way. A lot of people sit on the fence with the idea that there is "something out there". Others have some sense of belonging to a faith, but in practice it's peripheral to their day-to-day lives. I grew up in a church which believed that God's power was for another age. God was real, but didn't do miracles anymore. Our job was to believe, try to be good and wait for heaven.

The churches I had belonged to in Sheffield were churches longing to see faith make an impact. In reaching out for a God we believed could change things, we sometimes made the mistake of making out it could be more straightforward than the facts we were seeing. If God's will was clear, then we just needed to believe. The question we would be forced to answer is: *what do you do when you believe and nothing changes?*

The basis of our prayers was the Word of God – what the Bible said and what we believed God was saying through prophetic words.

A while into Ben's treatment another Christian couple and their son appeared on the ward. They too came from a church that believed God healed and had people praying. However, unlike us, they believed that to know their son would be healed they needed a prophetic word from God to say so. I thought they were plain wrong. I knew it was God's will. God hadn't made Ben sick and would make him better.

The first weekend we were in hospital with Ben, a guest arrived at our church to lead the service. He knew nothing of Ben's condition, which had only come to light two days earlier. With him he brought a picture he believed God had shown him of a father's hand reaching down to a child. At the time, the former Pastor of the church felt God was saying that he was going to take Ben home. He didn't feel he should share this at the time.

Looking back, I wonder if people should have broached the question of Ben's possible death earlier. Ultimately, it's not a big issue – we would have prayed come what may and people's support for us was magnificent. I don't believe people could have done any more. I don't look back and believe people were at fault. I do look back and think my theology, my way of understanding God, was at fault.

Another significant prophecy came from someone who didn't know us, but had heard about Ben and was praying:

As I was listening and praying, I felt God ask me to pray that it would snow over Ben. This caught my attention as I thought it was a very strange thought and an odd thing to pray! I felt God was asking me to consider what snow is (it's water in frozen form, I thought) and what effect it has. The latter I considered on and off at different points: For me, snow has the impact of being very beautiful in the way that it covers everything in sight. It causes noise to be dampened and I've always kind of loved the way it causes the world (or this country!) to stop, and life is taken at a different pace with the disruption. I considered the way many plants die off during the winter and lots of unwanted "bugs" do as well, and how you can think that some plants in your garden have totally died off, but come spring time they've obviously been safe underground and start bearing amazing flowers.

In relating this to Ben, I am praying that if this is God's message to him and his family, He will confirm it to them, either through other complementary/comparable words or a deep sense for them that this is from Him. I know I don't always get it spot on, so I don't claim to!

I think that this relates to Ben in the following ways:

- I believe God plans to cover the whole situation with His power and His peace – that the WHOLE situation would be impacted by Him and His will for it – that nothing will be missed

- I believe that God plans to kill off the tumour, the unwanted "fruit"
- I believe that God plans to restore Ben's optic nerve – that while it lays "dormant" underground it is safe and the fruit of this will be seen in the "spring"
- God is in the HUUUUUGE disruption that this is causing in Ben and his family's life and will bring many good things out of it

Again, clearly this was a huge encouragement. God knew what was happening, God would sort it out and, more than that, turn it into something positive. We prayed for Ben to be fully healed, the first of many to be healed as the word got out.

When Ben had lost his sight following his first chemotherapy, he had appeared depressed, becoming uncharacteristically subdued. The problem reoccurred during the next course as the chemotherapy caused swelling, which pressed on the optic nerve. This time Ben's response was different: he just replaced his eyes with his mouth and talked incessantly. This meant that at any time of day or night Ben could be heard on the ward, or the sound could be heard of someone reading him a story. He loved stories, especially Mr Gum and Roahl Dahl. Despite being stuck in hospital for days at a time with poor or no sight, he was brave and upbeat. When he was well enough he also enjoyed visits to the school classroom where he was fantastically looked after, forming close bonds with one of the teachers, Rachel.

Rachel was full of creative ideas of things for Ben to do. We still have a huge model of a dinosaur they made together. If Ben couldn't get to the classroom, the classroom would come to him. Rachel would arrive with a big smile and a tray full of sand or ice cubes or recording equipment. It was very distressing to hear at one point that funding was due to be cut and Rachel would be leaving. Louise didn't take this lying down and one day at home I had an odd moment when a load of senior council colleagues from the Children's Department trooped into our house to be given a dressing down by Louise.

Ben, like Louise, was an extrovert, while me and Joe are the resident introverts, happy to find our own space. Ben didn't appear to reflect much, he just got on with things. However, one day I got a call from Louise at work. She told me Ben had asked her what heaven was like, because he didn't want to die. Later we talked, flat and scared and decided that we would pray every night and invite others who could join us to do so. We put the following post on Facebook:

Ben came home on Monday. He is on good form, but his eyesight is sporadic and weak. A few things this week have hit home in terms of what we are facing and our response is to make sure we are on the front foot in terms of prayer.

As part of this we are going to have a day of prayer and fasting on Friday. If you could join with us in that, in any way, that would be great. Fasting is nothing magical, but frees up some time and attention to focus on prayer. If you want to join with us it's up to you what you fast and for how long.

Ben's tumour is aggressive in terms of its growth so our response is to be aggressive in prayer. We believe we are in a spiritual battle and it's not a matter of persuading God to act, but praying against the devil's work. James 4:7 says, *"Submit yourselves to God. Resist the devil and he will flee from you."*

To get a flavour of how we are praying, we are,
- Praying life, strength, blessing, growth, productivity and functionality to Ben's brain and especially his sight
- Praying death to the tumour, an end to growth and swelling, for it to shrink, shrivel and disappear

A few years ago we went to Spain and had some bags stolen in the airport. When we got to where we were staying, we found this out and found even our newspaper had been taken. I went to our room and told the devil that I wanted everything back. The next day we went to the airport and got everything back, even the newspaper. That's how we're praying here. We are not accepting the cancer and are not willing for anything to be taken from Ben; not his life, his eyesight, his hormones, his ability, his education, his potential, his future, his hope.

The other day Ben was singing the old classic, *I get knocked down, but I get up again, you're never going to keep me down*. Let's have that as his anthem

One of our key prayer supporters was our friend, Alistair, who had started a church a few miles from us. One night he came and read a Bible passage from the book of 1 Samuel chapter 30. It tells the story of King David returning home to find his camp has been ransacked. God tells him to pursue his attackers and he will get everything back:

"David enquired of the Lord, 'Shall I pursue this raiding party? Will I overtake them?' 'Pursue them,' he answered. 'You will certainly overtake them and succeed in the rescue.' David recovered everything the Amalekites had taken, including his two wives. Nothing was missing: young or old, boy or girl, plunder or anything else they had taken. David brought everything back." (1 Samuel 30)

That became a key prayer for me. We were seeking everything back: Ben's health, his sight, his hormone functions, his ability to reproduce. We prayed for a long, full life, including a full head of ginger hair. One time as I prayed I got a picture of the graphics bar you get when a computer file downloads as it goes from 0% to 100%. I prayed for a 100% download of healing.

The coming weeks brought a lot more discomfort for Ben and slog for me and Louise, but we got a sense that the tide was turning as we got a series of good results.

The first was another CT scan, which showed that the chemotherapy was successfully reducing the size of the tumour and that it appeared to be breaking up. This was the first good news in terms of the cancer and we had been told the radiotherapy, which was to come, was generally more effective. Our prayer was that these treatments would mean there was no need for the high-dose chemotherapy.

The next good news was the levels of a stem cell harvest. Ben was connected to a machine for several hours, which took out blood and harvested the white blood cells. These could then be given back when Ben needed them later. We told people to pray for a result of eight, which would be hard to get. In the end they harvested a ten!

Towards the end of July we had a push on praying for Ben's sight. I gave photos of Ben to people who were at our house praying and asked them to speak to his eyes and command sight. Soon after, Ben went to the park across from the hospital with a friend and Louise clearly saw him flinch when his friend ran by. Ben was able to explain in the coming days that he could see shapes. His mobility clearly improved as his confidence in making out things around him grew. We started setting prayer targets and were delighted as Ben could see colours and read big words. I was convinced we were seeing a miracle unfold. What we, or rather Ben, was seeing, was far more than we'd been told to expect the day after the fit when we thought Ben would be blind for life.

During the summer Ben started getting frequent swelling around his head. A few times we had to take him into the hospital to get checked over. I remember taking him in the middle of the night. We had to wait a couple of hours to see the on-call consultant who said we could go home. There were a series of Facebook posts about the swelling and concern grew that the bone flap where Ben's skull had been lifted for surgery would have to be removed to be replaced later with a metal plate. As much as we would have accepted this, had it been advised, we were praying to take everything back and we didn't want this. Over time the threat and the swelling receded. One day we left the hospital in the rain after the all-clear regarding the swelling. As we loaded Ben into the car we saw a double rainbow. We saw rainbows as a sign of God's promise, just as He had sent one to Noah when promising the earth would never flood again. We were going to get our promise; we would take everything back. That is the book I wanted to write: "Taking Everything Back – the story of overcoming childhood cancer".

More good news followed. Ben's level of cortisol had improved until he no longer needed to take hydrocortisone – something we thought he might need for life.

We had many positive signs and answers to prayer over these months. One time Louise and I took Ben to a little theme park in Derbyshire and as I helped Ben onto a ride he banged his head on a metal guard rail. I was devastated as we'd had so many issues with swelling. We prayed and Ben felt okay to carry on and take in all the rides. We even bumped into one of Ben's nurses who thought he seemed fine. At the end of the day we remembered the incident and realised there wasn't a bruise, not even a scratch.

At the end of chemotherapy a scan showed the cancer had reduced to a crust on Ben's nerves. Ben's consultant was delighted. It was as good as she could have expected with radiotherapy to come. But it was still there. That meant Ben would need the high dose treatment.

* * *

Radiotherapy began in September. Ben's treatment left him with little energy, so he was transported around in a buggy. It was strange to go back to a buggy and nappies, having thought those days were well behind us.

Another symptom we had been warned of was a lack of appetite. Ben was famous for having an excellent appetite and had a bit of a tum. Now it was a challenge to get him to eat and drink and at times he needed overnight hydration to avoid getting dehydrated.

Ben had 44 sessions of radiotherapy at Weston Park Cancer Hospital, which was just up the road from the Children's Hospital. Staff at both hospitals had developed excellent techniques for helping the children to manage the treatment. Ben had to lie face down, with his head covered by a special mask and keep still for five minutes at a time while he was zapped by a huge machine. He was given a piece of ribbon to hold, which stretched across the room and under the door to where Louise was. If he needed reassurance he could tug on the ribbon. No one else could be in the room because of the radiation, but he could listen to music, so every day he would be helped along by a children's worship

CD. Ben handled all of this brilliantly. The treatment led to burns on his now hair-free head, which we treated by lathering him with cream. The staff at Weston Park were great. They made a real fuss of Ben. When his 6th birthday came they had a box of presents for him.

Staff in these kind of circumstances have a choice how emotionally involved they become with the children. It's understandable that some keep their distance and just do their job. Death is a regular feature of cancer treatment. We experienced the sickening shock on the ward when another child died. Getting emotionally involved means risking greater pain when a child dies. There are people who take that risk again and again to give their best to the children and families involved. These people will always stay in our memories. We did ask the staff to give us their memories of Ben after he died and didn't get a response. Maybe that was asking too much.

Knowing that the radiotherapy would weaken Ben further we decided to have a little birthday party for him before the treatment began. It was one of Louise's many good calls. When the treatment ended we had a month before the high dose was due. Much as we longed to know the cancer had been blasted away, Ben couldn't have another scan because the effects of radiotherapy continue for several weeks after it has finished.

In our few weeks off we had a trip to Legoland with money that friends from church had raised by doing a car wash. This was another wonderful act of kindness among many. It became clear early on that we would never be able to properly thank people for the way they threw themselves behind us. I can only say that we were, and are, profoundly grateful and it was this support that saw us through. We saw families in the hospital coping alone, some having to travel from miles away to get to the hospital. It helped us massively that we were only a couple of miles away and had such faithful support.

We had a great time at Legoland. We booked a posh hotel with Joe relishing the challenge of seeing how much he could eat every morning at the buffet. We had two days at Legoland going on all of the rides with Ben's buggy proving extremely useful at beating the queues. Ben loved rides – the bigger the better. It was his job to look after Louise, who was a lot less keen. At the end of our first day there was a big fireworks display set to music. The bright fireworks set against a dark sky meant Ben could clearly enjoy the show and he stamped his feet along to the music. It was a very emotional time to see Ben so visibly enjoying himself.

November came and so did the high-dose treatment. This meant being in isolation in his room, with no visitors apart from close family. We had been warned from early on that this was a high-risk, unpleasant treatment. Louise had always been worried about it, but to be honest a mix of faith, optimism and denial meant that I was convinced it would be okay. My logic was simple: it had to be, Ben just had to get better.

Chemotherapy stops cells growing so it can stop the cancer growing. As well as hair cells it affects the skin, so Ben got cracked lips, mouth ulcers and a sore throat. After the treatment his mouth was full of mucus he couldn't swallow. Nights in hospital were spent with Ben constantly coughing up mucus. We had prayed against infection, but we found he had got a couple of bugs in his system including RSV. For a healthy adult this is just a cold, but to those who are vulnerable it can be very dangerous. Over a period of days Ben's breathing got worse and he started to need oxygen. We were forever asking to see doctors and he had a number of chest X-rays. We didn't realise until later that these are always a couple of days behind in the picture of the lungs they give. We were told Ben's lungs were okay, but he didn't seem anywhere near okay.

One day at work I got a call to say Ben's white blood cell count was improving well. We were delighted, thinking this indicated that his strength to fight things off was coming back. In fact it meant his body had started to try and fight the infection, but it wasn't strong enough.

The next day Louise rang to say that Ben had been taken into Intensive Care. I was only twenty minutes away and was still confident that a little time on a respirator would sort things out. That night things seemed settled enough for me to go home, but Louise's mum stayed at our house in case I needed to leave in a hurry.

The call came at 5.00am. Ben's condition had nosedived.

The nurses had tried to move Ben and his oxygen saturation rate had gone dangerously low. We became very aware of Ben's oxygen saturation rate over the next two months. This should normally be in the high 90s out of 100. For a healthy person it would go down after vigorous exercise, but soon recover. Ben needed to be in the 90s, minimum 88. He was struggling to keep to this rate with the respirator on full blast.

At 7.00am we spoke with Ben's cancer consultant who warned us that Ben could die that day. We asked friends to come and pray and sat around feeling desperate and hopeless.

Around mid-morning I decided I had to do something and went into Ben's room to pray. I prayed angry prayers demanding recovery. This was not about twisting God's arm, but about speaking to the sickness from the devil that was afflicting my son. In the name of Jesus I sought to take authority over the sickness. As I prayed, the numbers improved. During this time I got a text from a friend saying he had a picture of Jesus sitting next to Ben with His hand on his chest and his breathing getting stronger. I felt God say that just as the earth is held by a gravitational pull, He was holding Ben. A friend from church said he believed this would be a day where we saw God's glory. Others joined me and things continued to improve, but then later they deteriorated again. Ben was clearly right on the edge.

At this point we decided to bring Joe up to the hospital to tell him what was happening. We didn't take him to see

Ben, as we didn't want the image he saw to be the one he remembered. I asked him to help us remember the good times. The three held of us each other and cried our hearts out. I think it was the first time that Joe realised Ben could really die.

At 4.00pm we went into a side room with Ben's cancer consultant and the Intensive Care consultant. The ICU Consultant told us straight that Ben had an extremely small chance of survival. They were expecting him to die.

I went into the toilet and told God that if He was real He'd better show up. Ben kept going. We kept praying. By now, in addition to the normal ventilator, he was on an oscillator, which was literally pumping air into his lungs like a booming speaker at a gig. On top of this he was having nitrous oxide. There was nothing more they could give him and Ben was not picking up.

At 10.00pm I was in Ben's room with his nurse and two friends, Alistair and Martin, who were praying. Louise was asleep outside, exhausted after not sleeping the night before. The nurse and a colleague attempted to move Ben's position. This was done to avoid bed sores. Ben's saturation rate dived and the crash team was called. The consultant came in and replaced the ventilator with a hand pump using a technique called bagging. This is more effective, but can only be done for short periods of time. We had been warned that if Ben's rate dropped to the 70s and 60s that he wouldn't recover. I remember Ben's numbers dropping to the 60s, 66 I think.

The consultant was working hard. She was calm, but it was clear in her eyes that she didn't hold out any hope. Ben was reconnected to the ventilator. I looked at my friends as if to say, "What's happening guys?" Outwardly, they too were calm. I have no doubt they were praying. At times, when Ben had been dipping in the past hours, I had found myself mixing prayers with calls to him to keep going. Now I had nothing left. I thought it was all over. I considered whether I should go and get Louise. I didn't know what to do. I stood and watched, waiting for the inevitable.

Then something extraordinary happened.

In all the time we stood staring at the machine, I never saw Ben's numbers increase quickly. It seemed to make sense that his lungs could deflate quickly as they failed, but couldn't inflate quickly.

In a couple of seconds I saw Ben's numbers leap to 94 then 97. I never got a medical explanation of how this could happen. Neither did anyone explain how Ben's lungs could switch from clearly failing to slowly, but steadily, improving.

Ben's saturation rate never again dropped to the same dangerous levels. Very slowly, over days and weeks, we saw improvement. The nitrous oxide and then the oscillator were removed. Eventually Ben came off the ventilator and then improved until he no longer needed oxygen.

My only explanation was, and is, that this was a miracle. Over time it became clear, sometimes from third parties, that there were staff in the hospital who had the same view.

I asked one of the Christian doctors if they had a medical explanation and didn't get one. Ben's nurse that night who cared for him many more times said he'd never known someone with that level of respiratory damage survive. A registrar told us they were amazed at the progress he had made. I talked about a divine kiss of life – then more than that, a sense that God had rebooted Ben's lungs.

Having warned us that Ben was likely to die, Ben's cancer consultant travelled the next day to a conference. When she came back she fully expected to be comforting us on our loss.

Ben made it and we are profoundly grateful, despite his loss, that he got through that time. As bad it was to lose Ben, we knew it would have been much worse to have lost him suddenly without warning, in surgery or in Intensive Care.

We got our miracle. We got some more time.

* * *

Ben was in Intensive Care for three weeks and in hospital for a three month stretch in all. Eventually, over a period of eight months, Louise and I must have spent four or five months in hospital.

In Intensive Care we were given a parents' room in the hospital, with a proper bed and its own bathroom. Intensive Care meant that Ben had 24-hour care, which meant when it was our turn to stay we could try and get a proper sleep. When we were on M3 we slept on a fold-up bed and were often woken to deal with Ben. We could be woken by him being sick, coughing up mucus, or having to change him. When we returned to the ward we could be woken by the alarm that went off if Ben's breathing rate dropped lower than it should, which meant he needed to be moved or encouraged to take a few big breaths. Other times Ben would just wake up and want a story, as he had no idea what time it was and wasn't much bothered. One small consolation for me was that the interactive TV system had Sky Sports on, so I was cheered up by watching England retain the Ashes and even watched the bizarre spectacle of my beloved West Ham beating Man United in the Carling Cup.

The prayer support in Intensive Care was phenomenal. On the day it looked like we would lose Ben, a group of friends stayed all day and a couple well into the next morning. People then organised themselves so that there would be a constant prayer presence twenty-four hours a day. This lasted for a week until it became clear Ben was going to make it. This prayer support meant that we could go to bed knowing not just that Ben had a nurse there, but also a friend praying. The hospital were completely supportive of this throughout.

At one point Louise and me both stayed in the hospital for several days because we had been snowed in. My mum had travelled up from Bristol and helped look after Joe. This brought back to mind the snow prophecy. Well, it certainly snowed and we were encouraged that having stared death in the face, Ben was going to overcome the attempt on his life.

We talked openly to the staff about our faith. I told the nurse who saw Ben at his worst that when Ben recovered we would have a big party and that he and all the other staff would be invited. I had it mapped out in my head. A booming X-Factor style announcement celebrating everything that Ben had come through (7 hours of surgery, 5 courses of chemotherapy, 44 doses of radiotherapy, etc). I thought about the music – "This could be the best day ever" from the *Phineas and Ferb* cartoon that the boys loved and "I gotta feeling, that tonight's gonna be a good night...". I pictured people cheering as Ben made it onto a stage. He would have lapped up the adulation.

But Ben was not out of the woods yet and remained in Intensive Care for several weeks. It took a while to know Ben would make it. His breathing slowly improved, but we were warned that the effects of the oscillator would leave his lungs damaged. One day his temperature shot up and his heart rate went up to 175. I couldn't see how his body could take it. He had cooling blankets put on him and things were brought under control. We had been sent out of the room and I remember pacing desperately. One of the staff nurses saw me looking anxiously through the window and swung the monitor round to show me that things had stabilised. I broke down with relief.

That day Joe came into the hospital.

He had written the following poem:

Peace and calm,
Joy and hope,
All of these do not cause harm,
So please try to use these holy symptoms everyday at work
or on holiday,
Do not go astray of God

Joe was having to cope with the complete loss of family life. He'd lost having his parents together, unless that was at the hospital. His brother had gone from his playmate of the past five years to a sick child in a bed. He coped amazingly well and we are very proud of him.

During all of his time on the ventilator, Ben had been sedated. He was fed intravenously, but was absorbing very little. Our chunky, lively little boy was thin and bony. He was covered in tubes with lines into his wrist and foot and groin to administer drugs. He had a catheter in his penis and a nappy on. He was surrounded by a wall of machines, which alarmed if a drug line was blocked or his breathing rate dropped. This would have been no way to see him go.

Ben eventually successfully came off the ventilator and was able to be brought round. He was desperately weak, but able to say, "Where's Joe?" and "I want doggy", his favourite cuddly toy.

Ben's breathing was still weak and he was on oxygen. His lungs were full of mucus that he was too weak to cough up.

I was in with him one day when I realised he couldn't cough up what he needed to. The crash team were called to suction the gunk up. This happened several times and, at one stage, Ben had to go back on the ventilator for a couple more days. All of this was scary and draining, but eventually Ben was able to go back down to the ward.

We were preoccupied with worries about Ben's breathing and it was hard not to be fixated on the breathing monitor. There were setbacks, but the improvement continued. Other progress was painfully slow. Ben had lost a lot of muscle definition. He started to have physio, including being strapped to a tilt table to start putting pressure on his legs. Then slowly they started to get him to stand and walk with a frame. He never walked by himself again.

As the breathing improved, the big issue became Ben being able to absorb food. This is what kept us in hospital well into the New Year. Ben just wasn't managing food through the tube well and so was constantly being sick. Again, this never got back to normal. One day, when Ben had come home, we took him to the Pets Corner at the Chatsworth Estate and he asked for a mini milk and finished it all. Another time after Ben had to have a general anaesthetic for a lung test called a bronchoscopy, Louise searched all the nearby shops for a rocket lolly he'd been promised. He managed a few licks and we got a lovely photo. The problem with Ben being sick was that it sometimes meant he vomited up his feeding tube. He then had to go and have a new one passed down, which he had to swallow. We always hoped it would be quick and successful and the doctor doing it would be nice. Most doctors were. One doctor, early on, was horrible when Ben was resisting having a thumb prick to get a blood sample.

Part of the challenge on the ward was that other than the consultants who you generally saw once a day on ward round, there were registrars who were only on a six-month training cycle and then, out of hours, just an on-call consultant. It's obviously easier to know who you're dealing with, but this wasn't always the case.

As concerned as we were, we were praying for and expecting progress and recovery. Ben could have visitors again and was delighted one day when some Sheffield United players came in to the ward. They were very taken with Ben and remembered him saying he needed a new shirt because his said "Ben 5" on the back and he was now 6. A few months later the captain, Chris Morgan, and another player, Andy Taylor, on a pair of crutches following an injury, came back with a "Ben 6" shirt.

We spent Christmas at the hospital with Joe on the camp bed and me and Louise on a mattress on the floor. It was not the most luxurious Christmas ever, but it was great to still have Ben and all be together. It was a month since we'd been told not to expect Ben to last the day. The hospital made a big effort to make it as special as they could, with lots of visits from Santa. In the afternoon we took Ben out for a walk in his buggy – the first time he'd left hospital in nearly two months.

For all of the stress of hospital life, there is as much sheer slog. There is a lot of frustration and waiting around as communication is often the thing that goes wrong. Louise became an expert on Ben's care and occasionally had to step in to make sure everything was happening when it should and as it should. There is also a lot of boredom and craving for home, as you constantly live out of a series of plastic bags. I have to say again, that Louise bore the brunt of all of this. She was effectively a full-time carer. It was unquestionably easier for me being at work, which was a welcome distraction with everyone around me cutting me all the slack I needed.

When one of us did get home of an evening, we would have a little time with Joe before getting him to bed. We would then have to get everything ready for the next day and sort anything out that needed doing in the house. During all of this we'd be talking to each other at the hospital to check progress. I used to crash and watch a bit of TV before going to bed and getting up early to get in and secure a parking space in the hospital car park. Louise's mum, who stayed with church friends nearby, would come early and take Joe to school.

A child getting cancer can ruin marriages. Frequent responses to losing a child are having another child or splitting up. Our marriage got stronger. This was partly because we'd already knocked plenty of corners off each other, establishing a pretty healthy marriage where we had learnt how to communicate well by initially communicating badly. We both instinctively knew we needed each other to get through this and had to sort out any tensions quickly as we went along. That's not to say it was all plain sailing, but the bottom line is that our marriage didn't wobble at any point.

I had planned to take Louise away for our tenth wedding anniversary. In the end I left ten minutes early that morning and got her a Sausage and Egg McMuffin on the way into hospital.

* * *

In February Ben had an MRI scan. This would tell us whether the cancer had gone. Following Ben's miraculous recovery in intensive care I was confident. Everyone was praying. It had to be clear.

We were taken down from the ward to the cancer clinic. Ben's nurse who was looking after him that shift came too.

The moment of truth.

"There is something on the scan."

Those are the worst words I have ever heard. There was a sickening inevitability about everything that followed.

There was no further treatment possible.

They were telling us Ben was going to die.

Ben had one centimetre of cancer and there was nothing the medical profession could do to stop it. Further surgery couldn't remove it all. Further radiotherapy wouldn't work as it hadn't worked already.

Our world fell apart. Friends came up to comfort us. No one could believe it.

The following day I went to the park across the road and lost it with God. I asked Him what He thought He was doing. How could this be happening?

I recall one of our key prayer supporters bewilderment as he drove to intensive care in November. "Why did you tell us we would take everything back if this is what's going to happen?"

I resolved to keep praying. One centimetre of cancer might defeat the medical profession, but could it really defeat God?

We kept praying. One of the members of the church stood at the front one day and declared that Ben would not die. We gathered church leaders to pray for Ben and against the spiritual attack on my church leadership. I did not want to consider that we would lose Ben.

At the follow-up meeting the day after the scan results we told the consultant that we wanted Ben home. We'd had enough of hospital. If they couldn't do anything more then we wanted to be together.

This meant being shown how to administer the drugs and feed. Louise was very good at all of this and kept a grid of drugs and times which guided our day-to-day life. She'd already learnt how to administer drugs into Ben's line so that we could be at home as much as possible. This was something which required great care to avoid Ben getting infections.

To begin with Ben was able to play and Louise's mum was always on hand to make up stories with his toys. As time went on, Ben spent more of his time on the sofa and eventually in bed as the cancer spread to his back and it hurt him to move around. It was hard to see Ben's strength and mobility fade, but it was good to be home together and surrounded by our own things. We had to go in weekly for a clinic appointment and outreach nurses came out to deliver supplies and check on how we were doing. As things progressed they came out more and more, especially to administer pain relief. They were always on hand, a great source of practical and emotional support.

We also got visits from Michelle, a fantastic outreach worker for children with sight problems. Whatever was happening with Ben she was able to engage him in having fun and learning. It meant a huge amount to us to see her investing in Ben and he continued to astound us with his intelligence and sharpness.

We received support from a number of cancer charities, one of which got us tickets to go and see Ben's favourite band, *Madness*. Louise made a few calls and persuaded them to let Ben meet the band, so he got to meet Suggs, hug Woody the drummer, and I got my 1982 Greatest Hits LP signed. We also took Ben's great friend, Grace, a fellow fan and daughter of our friends, Martin and Lindsey, who were real lynchpins for us throughout.

When the scan results came through I rang Sheffield United and Ben was able to be a mascot at the next home game. As we took him down to the pitch, *Madness* boomed out of the tannoy. They looked after us brilliantly, including giving Ben a hospitality box so he could rest.

Around this time Ben came down with shingles. This led to weeks of agonising nerve spasms, made worse by the fact that Ben's short term memory was now poor and he couldn't remember and understand what was happening.

A couple of weeks after we took Ben home, my denial slipped and it hit me that we might really lose him. I scrambled to write down some favourite memories. Louise accepted the reality of Ben's situation before me. Ben was deteriorating; movement became more and more painful for him.

My last ditch prayer attempt was to make a list of symptoms and the progress we wanted to see, to "pray them in". Top of the list was to hear Ben laugh again. He did soon after, but on the whole the symptoms failed to match my prayers. We tried to take Ben out a few times, but soon he wasn't even coming downstairs. I wince to think of the times I encouraged Ben to try something – to walk a few steps, to come downstairs on his bottom. I so wanted to see that he was getting better. But that was for my benefit, not Ben's. He wasn't getting better.

At the end of March, Ben went to hospital for the last time. I went for a walk to pray before it was time to go. I saw the clouds passing overhead, making shadows on the ground. It struck me that only God could make those clouds. Surely God, the Maker of heaven and earth, could intervene.

We were told the cancer was advancing rapidly. It was in his spine, which explained his reluctance to move around. We were warned that Ben had 4-6 weeks. He lasted a month.

We had thrown the kitchen sink at praying for Ben. We were desperate, there was no other hope. We had kept posting on Facebook and gathering people to pray. In the past months we had driven Ben to a festival in Lincoln and a local healing service to be prayed for, and others came to the house to pray, including an African Bishop who was visiting a church in the city. Our neighbours must have been a bit bemused by the convoy of sharp-suited Africans arriving. The Bishop prayed with compassion and I felt the presence of the Holy Spirit. Downstairs he said simply, "We pray, then it's up to God."

When his final scan was negative we took the decision that there would no more praying out loud over Ben, though people could come and pray quietly. We decided that all we wanted was for Ben to feel safe, comfortable and loved. He slept more and more, with us reading him stories and playing him music when he wanted it.

We knew it was just a matter of time.

Chapter Four
The End

~~~

As Ben became more poorly and needed more and more pain relief, we decided to visit the nearby Children's Hospice, Bluebell Wood, to see if it was somewhere that could help us.

Joe came with us and none of us were prepared for what we found. It helped that it was a beautiful day, but we were bowled over by what a lovely, well-designed place it was. Joe loved the playground and was more than happy with the idea of going for a stay

The hospice was only a twenty minute drive away, just outside Sheffield. The building was only a few years old, with all of the bedrooms facing out into the garden. Inside there was a large lounge full of sofas and toys with big tables where staff joined families to eat great food cooked by their own chefs.

We decided to go and see if it worked for us. For Ben to be comfortable enough to travel he had to be pumped full of steroids, which sent him a bit hyper. I went with Ben in the ambulance, which was a challenge because he wriggled on the bed until he was sideways and I was left holding his head in my hands. Being at Bluebell meant that all of Ben's medical care was taken out of our hands. Staff stayed in with him at night and read to him if he woke up. Louise and I had our own room. So did Joe and so did Louise's mum and her husband, Brian.

Very soon we decided that we would stay at Bluebell until Ben died. I understand that some people want to be at home, but Bluebell allowed us to just be parents and get some rest. Ben couldn't see by now and wasn't that aware of where he was. All of the staff at Bluebell did an amazing job of looking after us. We had two cooked meals a day and when Ben was asleep we were able to go for walks in the countryside nearby. There was a mini heat wave and every morning we woke up to sunshine. It felt like the world's most surreal holiday camp.

The set-up at Bluebell meant that whole families could visit, as there was so much space and things for children to do. There was one unfortunate visit, when a lady we knew from a Sheffield prayer initiative came with a friend who had heard about Ben. Her friend decided it was appropriate to try and explain her theology of healing to us and pray over Ben. It was incredible that she thought it was appropriate to visit people in a hospice and do this, disregarding where we were and the journey we'd been on. At times like this the idea that it is always God's will to heal starts to resemble the story of King Canute ordering back the waves.

The staff did everything they could to make Ben's time special. A member of staff dressed up as the Easter Bunny and paid Ben a visit. The music therapy lady brought in musical instruments and a video camera, so we had some footage of Ben joining in songs with a shaker. Ben's nurse brought one of the hospice guinea pigs into Ben's room so that he could stroke it. We also had a special time in the hospice's sensory room, where we were able to get Ben comfy on a beanbag as we listened to *Madness*. We knew there wouldn't be many more times like this.

That was Thursday April 28th. Ben was still able to chat away and I had precious moments lying next to him on his bed and having a chinwag. We had a lovely surreal conversation, which we filmed, where we talked about being in a band. I said I couldn't play any instruments, so I would have to play the "air guitar", which Ben decided should be called a "false guitar".

That night Louise had a special moment holding Ben as his bed was changed. At one point he turned to her and said, "Do you like this smile, Mummy?" and pulled his biggest smile. This made a very special final photo.

Friday April 29th was the Royal wedding. We brought Ben out into the lounge on his bed, but he slept most of the day, waking occasionally and talking briefly a few times.

That evening Ben's nurse told us his breathing had

changed. At this stage the end didn't appear imminent, so we went to bed with the understanding that we'd be woken up if things changed.

They came for us at 5.00am. Ben's breathing was more laboured. We knew the cancer's advance was going to knock out different brain functions and eventually the messages to Ben's lungs would stop.

The staff had talked about making Ben's death as special as possible. As much as this sounds a contradiction, this wasn't losing Ben to surgery or in intensive care. This was as good a place as it could be. Ben was put on a double sofa bed and Louise and I lay next to him and played his favourite music on his iPod.

As the end drew closer, Louise, her mum, and I took the chance to hold Ben in our arms for one last time.

At about 3 o' clock on April 30th, Ben died.

He had lived 6 years, 7 months and 8 days. He had squeezed everything out of his life that he could. Nowhere near long enough, but too precious for words.

Chapter Five
Saying Goodbye

~~~

We had some time holding Ben, but not too long as we needed to wash him before the effects of death took hold on the body. So we washed our son for the last time. As we did, we looked at his body thinking how well he looked. He wasn't skinny and he had definitely grown. We dressed him in his Ben 10 pyjamas and took him down to the Forget Me Not Suite.

This was a room with a bed for Ben, where people could go to see him and say goodbye. The room had a cord you could pull to put cooling air in, so that he could stay there for longer. Attached to the room was a separate bedroom and lounge if family wanted to stay close.

Joe wasn't around the day Ben died, as it had been arranged for him to be with our friends, Brian and Donna, Ben's godparents. They brought Joe back that night. We told him Ben had died and he went down to see him. The end was a big shock for everyone and there were plenty of tears, but we were as prepared as we could have been and felt in the best place possible to cope.

I've heard of churches sending deputations to pray for people to be raised from the dead. We didn't have the energy or faith for that. It felt as though if God had wanted to restore Ben He'd had plenty of chances. I did visit once and pray for Ben to be raised myself, mostly so that I didn't have the risk of regretting not having done so. I didn't feel I had anything to lose.

We believed that Ben was now in heaven, free from pain. Months later in church I had a picture of Ben with Jesus' arm around him. I know for some people this is sentimental twaddle, but to me death, like birth, is a time that makes me feel that life is more than a series of biological incidents.

A couple of days after Ben's death I woke up with a real sense of peace and a huge amount of pride. Ben had coped and fought magnificently, displaying dignity and courage way beyond his years. The book of Philippians in the Bible talks about life being like running a race. Ben's race had been way too short, but still remarkable and unforgettable. He had touched many lives, left many friends. As the days and weeks went by we saw the genuine impact his life had had, and we know continues to have.

In all of this, there was relief. We had been through an incredibly traumatic year, living on adrenaline. We were exhausted. It was over.

Ben's service gave us a focus for the coming couple of weeks. A church, St Thomas' Philadelphia that we had links with, agreed to let us use their large city centre building, so we knew we could fit everyone in. We had no idea how many people would come, as so many people had been involved in Ben's battle in some way.

Organising the service brought out the best in Louise in many ways. We had a meeting with people from Philadelphia to run through the service. I was struggling to think straight, but Louise kept things together and had a series of creative ideas to make the service special.

The children from Ben's class wrote down special memories of Ben and stuck them on butterflies, which were displayed at the back of the room where we had the service. We know that no one in Ben's class will forget him. We gave all of them one of Ben's teddies to look after with a special message.

A local sawmill gave us a nice piece of wood and etched it with our new slogan for Ben: "Ben Luck, Keeping Jesus Busy". This travelled in the hearse with Ben's coffin and we left it on his grave.

We also produced mugs with a picture of Ben and the phrase, as well as some words from the Gospel of John (chapter 14, verses 1 and 2), which were read at the service:

"Do not let your hearts be troubled. Trust in God; trust also in me. In my Father's house are many rooms; if it were not so I would I have told you. I am going there to prepare a place for you."

We sold the mugs and gave the proceeds to Bluebell.

We were moved by the support we had throughout from the boys' school, St Joseph's. It's a small Catholic school with only one class per year, which makes it a very close school. St Joseph's Catholic Church is next to the school and, despite the fact that we are not Catholics, the Priest agreed to have Ben buried in the church yard. Not only this, but they buried him in a section next to the church with past Priests, the greatest honour in death they could give Ben.

On the day of Ben's service we walked the short distance from our house to the church behind the hearse with *Madness* playing at full blast. The funeral directors had arranged for Ben to be in a lovely bright green coffin, his favourite colour.

As we approached the church we saw the faces of our friends creased with grief. I just couldn't look at people. Our friend, Ray Booth, a retired church leader, had agreed to take the service. At the grave he lay Ben to rest with a few simple prayers. Words cannot describe how sickeningly surreal it is to bury your child. It's just not what's supposed to happen.

The church put out 500 seats and the building was full. Friends and family came from around the country and many people came from St Joseph's. We asked people to wear green as it was Ben's favourite colour.

We showed a PowerPoint montage of pictures of Ben set to the *Athlete* song, *Black Swan* – a beautiful song from one of our favourite bands, which seemed incredibly fitting and poignant:

I've been racing the clock and I've run out of steam
I am ready for my final symphony
Oh, my body is weak but my soul is still strong
I am ready to rest in your arms

We sang some of Ben's favourite songs. Ray spoke with a gentle but firm compassion about the reality that we all die and that in God we can find an eternal perspective on the bewildering present. Near the end of the service our friend, Giles, read a section of one of Ben's favourite books – *The Giraffe, the Pelly and Me* by Roahl Dahl. We had listened to and read the story many times. The ending always seemed sad, as the boy had to leave. As Giles explained:

After Ben lost his sight, one of his favourite things was listening to stories, either on CD or having someone read to him. We're fairly certain that he's one of the most well-read 6-year olds in heaven. He loved lots of different books, but one of his favourite authors was Roald Dahl. He knew the books so well that if, while you were reading, you pronounced a name wrong or made any other mistakes, he would correct you.

A story that Ben knew well from being a toddler is *The Giraffe, the Pelly and Me*. It's the tale of a young boy called Billy who makes friends with the Giraffe, the Pelly (a pelican) and the Monkey from the Ladderless Window Cleaning Company. They have a fantastic adventure whilst cleaning windows at the Duke's house. They catch a burglar stealing the Duchess's jewels, which earns them great rewards.

I'm going to read you the end of the story. Billy is about to say goodbye to his friends.

"I've got to leave you now," I said. "I must go and look after my customers in the shop."

"We must go too," said the giraffe. "We have one hundred windows to clean before dark."

I said goodbye to the Duke, and then one by one I said goodbye to the best three friends I had ever had. Suddenly, we all became very quiet and melancholy, and the Monkey looked as though he was about to cry as he sang me a little song of farewell:

"We have tears in our eyes,
As we wave our goodbyes,
We so loved being with you, we three,
So do please now and then,
Come and see us again,
The Giraffe and the Pelly and me.
All you do is to look,
At a page in this book,
Because that's where we always will be,
No book ever ends,
When it's full of your friends,
The Giraffe and the Pelly and Me."

Standing in front of everyone and holding myself together enough to pay tribute to Ben is the hardest thing I have ever done.

What follows is the tribute me and Louise gave:

Over the past few weeks people have said a lot of kind things to me and Louise. People have said we've been brave, heroic, even inspirational. We don't feel like that; we've just done our best to keep going. The thing that has helped us to do that has been the love, practical support and prayer of the people around us. That is what has kept us afloat. So if you want to be inspired by something, be inspired by that, by what happens when people get behind something and don't give up because that's something we can all do again.

Today is a day we never wanted to happen. We are heartbroken to have lost Ben, but at the same time we find we still have much to be thankful for. We want to thank everyone for coming today; the support we have had over the past year has been phenomenal. I need to mention two people who have walked every step of the way with us. Louise's mum, or Big Nannie to give her proper title, got the first flight over and has been with us the whole time, doing anything she could to help. Thank you. Joe has been an amazing big brother. We want you to know we love you and couldn't be more proud of you.

It's fitting we are not at our church today, but another

in the city, because we have had huge support from the church in the widest sense. To those involved in the church, we have been able to say to people, "This is what the church is supposed to be about." We have had massive and faithful prayer support over the past year and are very aware that this is continuing. At times in Intensive care, we had people in Ben's room praying round the clock and Ben made a miraculous recovery, which gave us 5 months more than we were expected to have. Our church, Living Waters, has operated as God's hands and feet, caring for us, including bringing us meals every night for months. The church in the city heard we had a problem with our heating system and gave money to have it replaced. The St Joseph's school community has also been a tremendous support to us all, putting faith into practice.

We want to thank everyone at the Children's Hospital for working so hard to try and get Ben better. When it became clear that Ben was going to die, we went to Bluebell Wood Hospice where everyone cared not just for Ben, but for us as a family. We want everyone to know that we believe everyone did everything they could for Ben.

There is no escaping the pain that we feel at losing Ben, but in the depth of that pain we see just how precious he was to us and we thank God that we had him in our lives.

We need to ask for your help today, and in the coming weeks and months, to remember Ben. This has already started, with some work his class at school has done that you can see later. We'd love to hear your memories and stories so we can put a book together. I want to ask you to picture Ben. It's hard and it often makes us cry, but we should smile too to think of the joy he brought us.

When I picture Ben I remember him in his green St Joseph's jumper. Ben loved school and I remember picking him up and him bouncing along to the car. I picture Ben as a blur of green and ginger running into the house.

I picture Ben is his blue swimming t-shirt. Ben loved water so much that we wondered if he'd been born with gills. On holiday, in France, two summers ago the sun shone every day and Ben spent hours in the pool.

You can't think of Ben for long without thinking of food. Ben's appetite was legendary. A few days after his big operation last year Ben was ready for something to eat. We asked what he wanted and he simply said, "burger". A big cheeseburger was ordered and disappeared very quickly.

When I think of Ben, I think of him smiling, jumping up and down with excitement, always in the thick of things at church gatherings. I think of Ben having adventures with Joe, playing *Star Wars* or *Thunderbirds,* or running around the house with walkie talkies. We remember Ben as bright and energetic. He used to read shop signs and billboards as we drove past in the car.

It's impossible to picture Ben without remembering him getting poorly. There was so much he couldn't do any more, but he never stopped being Ben. Even in the last two weeks of his life at the hospice Ben was known for being bright, funny, inquisitive, articulate and polite. During Ben's illness we also saw new things – a great bravery and an amazing strength of character. Two days after he died I woke up and felt a great sense of pride at how Ben had coped throughout his sickness.

The last picture we have of Ben was taken two days before he died. Ben didn't move much because it was uncomfortable for him, but we had to get him out of bed to change the bed. Louise held Ben and as she did Ben said to her, "Mummy, do you like this smile?" and did a series of big smiles. That could be the last image we're left with, but that's not how we want to leave things.

I want you to picture Ben with a full head of ginger hair, with sparking eyes and a big smile, running around having fun. Ben had a simple but very real belief in Jesus and we believe he is with Him in heaven now. So we have a new catchphrase for our gorgeous Ben, who we loved having with us and miss so much: *Ben Luck – Keeping Jesus busy.*

Chapter Six
What Happened Next?

~~~

On the first birthday after Ben died, lovely friends of ours bought us an apple tree to remember him. We planted it in the garden. It did well and yielded a fine crop. A couple of years on we decided it was time to move house again.

We'd already had the trauma of trying to dig up an olive tree given to us on Ben's dedication. We thought we'd killed it by not getting enough of the roots out and the apple tree felt like a job too far. But then the guys who'd bought the house said they'd dig it up for us and a while later they texted to say that they had.

Their intentions were good, but when we turned up we found the tree had few roots and was sat dried out in a cracked pot. Louise was devastated. We resolved to get it home and try and replant it. I grappled it into the car with a heavy heart and the following week in the driving rain we dug as deep a hole as we could to give it a new home. We held out little hope that it would survive.

One day, a few months later, Louise was leaving for work, but decided to take a couple of minutes to water the plants first. She burst back in to say that Ben's tree was alive. When I ventured down to see, I found that its branches were displaying many small buds.

It felt like a powerful metaphor. There was new life where we expected only death.

* * *

As I write, we are approaching the 5th anniversary of Ben's death. A huge amount has changed in our lives. We have moved house, changed church, Joe has changed schools, and Louise and I have had a series of job changes. It has been hard. We are not the same shape family we once were. Grief can sneak up and overwhelm us, but we have found that life can be good again and we are aware of being blessed in many ways.

The point of writing Ben's story was to say what happened next; to talk about how we were flung into a totally new place and how we coped and tried to make sense of that. We don't need to find ways to pay tribute to Ben. He is indelibly marked on those he met and, sadly, those he never met won't get to know him by reading a book. The question is, what do you do when the worst thing imaginable happens, when something so precious is taken away? What do you do and what does it mean for people who say they live by their faith like we did?

We have found that faith cannot stay the same. That is threatening to some. After all, the Bible says, *"Jesus Christ is the same yesterday, today and forever."* You'll find I still believe that, but anyone with faith interprets that in some way as they go along. It's that interpretation, that understanding – theology to give it its posh name – that has changed.

The good news is that this is not a theological book. As friends have patiently read the many versions of this book, I have been reminded to just tell the story. The second half of this book tells the story of how we learned to live again and how faith fitted into that. And that is one of the key points – belief in God is not something to be pondered philosophically when we find time. It's wrapped up with the business of living day to day, and our faith in God helps us with that, even in the midst of pain and confusion.

The question is how we deal with awful suffering like the kind we faced. It's not that we have cracked it and can offer a "how to" guide. We have learned some things about dealing with suffering the hardest way possible. We hope that sharing the story will be of help to others. Few people will have to go through what we did, but nobody is immune from suffering; tragedy reaches us all at some point. My hope is that writing this book helps those of us who are part of the church to have honest conversations about suffering, particularly what we do when we don't get the breakthrough or the victory that we hope for. I want readers who aren't a part of the church to know that God offers hope within our suffering, even if He won't always remove it the way we want. I believe authentic faith offers something unique to help us deal with our struggles.

The following chapters talk about how we coped and began to process losing Ben. In each chapter I have highlighted the sentence, or section, which best sums up that part of the journey. First I'll talk about the aftermath, the time of shock that we found ourselves in. Out of that we chose to still believe and to go back to church. I'll talk about what that was like and how that belief has changed in the light of the questions and pain that followed Ben's death. This belief has been at the heart of finding a "new normal", where we are learning how build a new life without Ben.

We get angry about suffering because we don't want it to happen. But it does anyway. Dealing with it forces us to look at life and, in our case, God differently. Through that we've found life isn't about happy endings or tidy solutions.

We've found that God doesn't stop life being messy,
He steps into the mess with us.

We didn't face our grief alone. We want other people to know they don't have to either.

Chapter Seven
Shock

~~~

A few months after Ben died we went back to the campsite in France where we'd all been two years before. This time we took the longer ferry to get a shorter drive. On the ferry journey home I decided to get some fresh air and walked out onto the open deck. I was all alone and on the other side of the guard rails was the big sea and oblivion. It was vividly clear just how easy it could be not to feel the pain anymore. I turned and walked back inside.

Louise and I both had these moments – moments where, with frightening clarity, we could see a way in which we wouldn't have to carry on. I am aware that it's a painful thing for those close to us to have to hear, but this wasn't about deliberation. We didn't have to weigh up the choices and find reasons to choose to carry on. It was more of a temptation not to have to. We steeled ourselves. We carried on.

* * *

Facebook post May'11:

We're doing okay on the whole. Joe has settled back into school. But the house is far too quiet and we miss having Ben around. We sit in his room and can't believe he's not there. At night, when we go to bed, he's not there to check on. The Thursday before Ben passed away, Bluebell Wood's music teacher made a video of Ben playing a shaker and tambourine. While Joe was on his tenor horn, she played piano and I strummed the guitar. Except Ben actually was more interested in chatting and asking questions. All of you who have spent any time with Ben in the last six months will remember this about him. Halfway through, spontaneously, Ben opens his eyes really wide, like he knows the camera is there, and does the biggest grin followed by a big toothy smile. We hadn't seen this on the day, so it was a lovely surprise to see it when we watched the DVD today. So difficult to believe that he was as bright as that just two days before he died. He was such a strong spirited, bright boy. A pure delight till the end.

* * *

What was it like? Looking back brings back emotions, events, glimpses.

The most obvious thing was that we were in shock and nothing felt normal. We'd had a year of "project Ben" – the mission to get him better and make him happy and comfortable. Now all that was finished and what was left was a gaping hole.

Our rhythm of life had become based on Ben and now he was gone and there was no way we could just pick up where we'd left off. Our world had been turned upside down by Ben's sickness and we had to figure out how to manage life without him, three rather than four, exhausted and traumatised.

We found ourselves living in a house where we'd never spent time together without that being based around Ben's sickness. The house was big and quiet. It had been bought to house a family centred around two young boys with space for them to grow up into men. Now, one of the rooms was empty.

I remember going with Louise to get Joe from school. He went back to his routine first. To begin with we'd go through the front entrance, not the school yard. Everyone was lovely, but we just couldn't manage that. We were trying to deal with our own emotions, we didn't have it in us to face other people's. We'd get Joe and go home and wonder what we were going to do for the rest of the day.

We felt a huge sense of emptiness, a raw ache of grief. Losing Ben was like losing a limb. There was a sense of yearning that was almost unbearable. Ben was a part of us, a child we had created, nurtured, shaped, delighted in. I felt misshapen without Ben. I was the father of two children. We had moulded our life around Joe and Ben – them as individuals and as a fantastic double act. I couldn't begin to imagine the pain for Louise, having carried Ben, given birth to him and then given herself, so completely, to his early years.

When we first lost Ben that's all there was and that's all we were. I remember thinking it was strange that there is no term for a bereaved parent – our culture's way of not having a description for the indescribable. There were moments of thinking that that was all I was now – the guy who had lost his son – that the enormity of losing Ben had swallowed up any other sense of purpose or identity.

You may look at trauma like this and think that you would flip out, shout and scream and smash things up. I know some people fear they would have a breakdown. We knew very clearly that we had to keep going for each other. At times the grief would surge; you could feel it like a wave coming in. When it came it would take over for a while until it was exorcised by tears.

The ache inside us was like a huge open scar from top to bottom, which the grief would tear open. Of course, this happened a lot because Ben was everywhere. There were his pictures, his things, all the memories. More than that, we'd had his presence for six and a half years and in that past year one of us, more often Louise, had been with him for all but a few hours. Every part of our lives were marked by his fingerprints. Now what?

At times I would need to look through pictures of Ben and have a good cry. Once in a while I would write a poem to try and express the emotional churning. After a while I realised they were all saying the same thing. Ben, how can you be gone?

Loss
A roomful of toys,
A houseful of photos,
A head full of memories,
A soul full of pain,
Why aren't you here?
Your smile,
Your contented face,
Your joyful laugh,
Your presence in the back seat,
Your hand on the journey to school,
So much missing,
A crater to navigate,
The loss that never ends

We may have looked like we had it together, but we didn't. One of my coping strategies for the pain was to swear repeatedly until I calmed down. I did this outside the florist in the days before Ben's celebration, having watched Louise hold it together enough to write the message for his flowers.

We so missed Ben and there wasn't a thing we could do about it. And what about anger? I'm sure we raged, but I don't remember a lot of that. Anger, like self-pity, wasn't going to be much help to our main objective of surviving and looking after each other.

Where I felt myself slip into depression and self-pity I bullied myself out of it. I knew I had to accept the reality of what had happened and learn to face it. I was scared of what would happen if I went downhill and knew that if I went off work with stress I might never return.

Some people said the way we dealt with things was, and is, inspirational. In truth that just feels odd. We plodded doggedly on. Lots of people helped us. Countless numbers were praying. We found ways to fill the time. Louise and I would often go out for local walks to clear our heads and talk. Joe became our focus and as his current passion was planes and helicopters, we went round a load of air museums and up in a few helicopters.

We needed friends and there were several families whose support made a huge difference. At church we met the Trails, an Australian family who were in Sheffield because Andrew was an eye surgeon on a two year fellowship. They were a riot! We saw them for lots of adventures, games and late nights.

The Webster's lived down the road. Louise and Jane had first met at a toddler group. They made us incredibly welcome at their place, which became like a second home.

Louise had been at University with the Scott's, who lived in Suffolk. Again, these guys treated us like part of the family, even letting us gatecrash one of their summer holidays. Our trips to see them were a big part of getting back on an even keel. All these guys were incredibly thoughtful and generous

– they weren't awkward with our grief and they helped us learn how to have fun again.

If you want to support someone facing tragedy, being available is the most important thing. You don't have to know what to do or say, because in these situations no one knows what to do. It's better to talk about it rather than avoiding it, because you fear saying the wrong thing. We want to talk about Ben. He is our son and we love him. However much it hurts, we cherish the time we had together and the amazing little boy he was.

I always tell people to offer help and let people say what is helpful. There is no point trying to second guess what your suffering friend needs – just ask them. One kind person emailed offering to bake some bread and bring it over, but I knew I didn't have the strength to see them so I emailed back our thanks and asked them just to pray. There were times I'd see people I knew in the shops and panic because I couldn't face them. I couldn't deal with the idea of saying how I was. I couldn't deal with seeing the pain and bewilderment mirrored back.

Back at school Joe was subdued. Like me, he tends to retreat into his thoughts. His school did a great job, providing stability and drawing him into a small group for those going through tough times. Joe was sad for all the things at school he couldn't share with Ben. Ultimately, he just got on with things. A couple of years later he found the guitar and poured all his energy into that.

Initially, I went back to work on a phased return. There was no pressure on me, I was given permission to do what I could. I covered a large part of the city and a few times took myself off to walk round it to get my head together. Over time I got back on my feet and was able to do a decent job. My team and managers were fantastic, carrying me initially and giving me space to regroup.

When I returned to work I chose to go and see a few key colleagues who I knew could bring me up to speed with things, while being able to cope with whatever state I would be in. Some other people didn't know how to face me. One begged my colleague to tell him what to say. What became hard was knowing when to tell others who didn't know about Ben. Sometimes, if people ask about my family I just tell them I have a son. Other people get the whole story. You sense some people won't know how to react, because it is always a shock to hear something so tragic.

Louise went back to teaching at the boys' school for a while, but knew she couldn't face teaching Ben's class, so she got herself back into secondary teaching. In the years after Ben died she has had a number of health issues, all of which led back to stress, depression and ultimately grief. The Children's Hospital Psychology team initially supported Louise with counselling sessions and, more recently, she has been supported by our GP and has started to take medication. Louise has mostly coped, not dealt with the grief. Afraid of not regaining strength and composure, she acknowledges that she chooses not to think about the pain of losing our son. As a result there are days when grief takes us by surprise and overwhelms us. There is no hiding from the force of that pain.

Unsurprisingly, Ben's illness and loss affects our everyday life, not just the significant dates, and for this we have to develop strategies for getting on with life. Getting to sleep is still an issue for Louise. She still has to use the Radio 4 iPlayer to get to sleep at night. There are places we choose not to visit and faces we find it hard to see without a bit of notice. Even church can be upsetting when a children's worship song is sung that Louise remembers from hospital during Ben's radiotherapy. So, in the day to day, trying to get on with our "new normal" life, we tend to deal with the moment, using a mixture of deep breaths, prayer and distraction to keep our thoughts from spiralling.

After Ben died, our great friend Alistair asked his friend Steve Redman to contact us. Steve had lost his son to cancer 10 years earlier and wrote a moving account called *At Least It's Not Raining*. Steve shared our pain and advised us that we needed to harness our emotion, so that it didn't consume us.

I threw my energy into writing. I wrote several children's stories, including one with Joe and Ben as characters. I also had a go at stand-up comedy, as strange as it must sound. I'd done a few open mic spots as an 18-year old and reading Michael McIntyre's autobiography I decided to try again. I did a couple of further open mics, including one at a fundraiser for the hospice. I didn't disgrace myself, but neither did any agents call. My curiosity had been satisfied.

Some people respond to a trauma like ours by throwing themselves into charity work. We had some involvement with the hospice for a while after Ben died, but ultimately found it easier to move away from that. We now live only half a mile from the hospital where Ben had all his treatment. We can manage to walk past it, but getting involved in anything to do with cancer would be too much. We found that after Ben died there were things we knew we couldn't handle. I had been involved in a number of leadership roles, all of which I gave up, most notably in our church.

One of the issues you face as a bereaved parent is the question of what could have been. I got a new CD by Nik Kershaw who had clearly just had another young child. The lyrics of one song – *The Sky's The Limit* – addressed to his young child hurt, as he sang about the potential of his life stretching ahead. The song spoke of all the things his child might be; that beyond being a President or a pop star, he could be amazing, funny and brave and lucky and glorious.

On the whole we have always tried not to go there. It's too painful to consider what might have been. I saw a boy from Ben's class on the bus one day and started picturing Ben playing football. So vivid. Other times I imagined getting off the bus at the stop for our old house, wishing that if I went back I'd somehow find him there. It is hard to see boys from Ben's class getting bigger and older.

Ultimately we have to deal with where we are, with *what is*, not *what if*. If that sounds trite, it's not. It's about survival; finding good things to help us deal with the new day.

To begin with we left Ben's room as it was. Sometimes we would sit on his bed and think about the times we'd shared. Slowly we worked through his things, resolving to keep what was most precious and give other things away. We wanted to remember, not create a shrine. At times we would face something one of us couldn't deal with. Louise had to close the drawer on Ben's school uniform. I couldn't face seeing one of his jumpers cut up to make a cushion. I needed to be able to pick it up and hold it. Louise did a lot of craft therapy, such as making old t-shirts into a blanket. We tried to use Ben's things to create positive memories, framing Ben's Sheffield United top and signed *Madness* t-shirt.

After a couple of years we took everything out of Ben's room and redecorated it. That way we had to think about what we could keep, and the best ways in which we could make those things a positive part of our home.

There's a lot of good stuff to treasure. We smile, but often with a lump in our throat. People know that memories are precious and they hope that memories will bring comfort. It's a tempting thought, but it misses the point. Ben is gone. The best memory does not bring him back. In our hearts we don't want to remember him, we want to experience him. Memories are a double edged sword and they are not Ben. Memories are precious, but they are not enough.

I remember seeing benches in the park across from the hospital and thinking, "I don't want my boy's name on a bench, I want him here with me." Now there is a bench with Ben's name on it at his school. A plaque on it says:

"Remember Ben with his ginger hair swishing; remember him, giggling, dancing and singing; he always had fun with his family and friends; now he's with Jesus where the fun never ends; Ben Luck – keeping Jesus busy."

Don't get me wrong, after his death I was glad for the bench, but we never wanted to be in that territory.

I can see Ben now. I can hear his voice, hear his laugh, imagine the softness of his skin, remember holding him and the way he would stick his bottom out and become a dead weight.

I can remember two Bens. The soft little cute boy with the tum and the mop of hair. Then there was the other Ben, lean, bald, stoic. What an amazing little boy he was. It takes my breath away to remember what he went through. Ben dealt with sickness head on, straightforward, every bit the Yorkshireman! We used to tell Ben we loved him a lot. Often he would just reply, "I know." I'm not sure I can think of a much better thing to hear as a parent.

There's a picture of Ben when he got home after surgery. He can still see to smile naturally. He still has a full head of beautiful ginger hair. He looks happy, relaxed, the most grown up he ever looked. We have these moments when there are no words, just tears, the lump to swallow. We see flashes of Ben everywhere and as we remember we cannot help but sometimes imagine the future that cannot be.

Sometimes I think about losing Ben in an almost factual way; other times the reality of it is like being punched in the face, such is the incomprehensibility of his absence. I am taken back there. My chest tightens, my throat hardens and I have to start thinking about my breathing and breathe and grimace and ride out the pain.

You can never get over the loss of a child, you have to learn how to live with it. Never think time fixes it. Never think things can go back to normal. Your suffering friend needs to know you are there for them and always will be.

The shock subsides, but it never leaves. We have had to get used to not having Ben around so that we can find a way to live without him. But at times the obscenity and ridiculousness of what has happened strikes again. How can this have happened? How can I have lost one of my three favourite people?

Over time the scar has healed and faded, but it will always be there throughout all that we are. At times something disturbs it and it opens up again. Ben's birthday and the anniversaries of his death are numbing. There are no words to capture it.

* * *

Facebook 1st Anniversary of Ben's death; April 2012
Our wonderful Ben, our hearts ache with the pain of

missing you. We still talk about your amazing memory, we tell folks who haven't met you yet that you were so intelligent, so articulate and well read. That you were loved by everyone who knew you; you had so many friends. You would have a go at anything and you always did your very best. You could eat a Happy Meal plus a McFlurry faster than a boy twice your age. You were funny and fun. You showed such determination and you were so brave. You did your best to get better, you had all that horrible treatment, went through a year of the worst that anyone could face and all with hardly a word of complaint. My heart can't stand to think of all that your little body suffered, my precious little boy. I wish that you hadn't had to go through all that. Sobbing as I type, be sure that my biggest wish is that you were still here with us now to share the bright future that should've been yours. We will ALWAYS love you x x x x

* * *

So we kept going, putting one foot in front of the other, dealing with one day and one thing at a time. We were forced to adapt to life without Ben. We learnt how to manage the pain and to try and see beyond it. We supported each other and we had great friends by our side.

We were learning how to live again, like a soldier in rehab awaking from surgery and trying to get themselves moving again.

The big question was always what do we do now? What do we do next? How do we keep going? Central to that was confronting the issues of our faith.

Chapter Eight
Choosing to Believe – Going Back to Church
~~~

A good while after Ben had died, Louise told me a story from before he was ill. Louise was suffering with depression at the time and had a routine of going to the gym and watching DVDs in the afternoon to distract her. One day she was at home watching the film *My Sister's Keeper*, about a child with a serious illness. Louise remembers the impact of seeing the child with a feeding tube up their nose. She'd also recently seen a film about the politician Mo Mowlam's life and sad death, detailing her huge change in personality after being diagnosed with a brain tumour. As Louise watched the film she felt God ask, "What would you do if that was your child? Would you still follow me?" The answer was yes. There was no question. It felt like a preparation, something that often came to mind.

* * *

We were Christians. That was completely central to who we were and how we lived our lives. Getting to grips with life again was going to involve dealing with faith and, more immediately, our involvement with church.

It wasn't that faith was a badge or a habit to us. It had shaped the people we were and the way we approached things. We did more than just to go church for an hour on a Sunday. Church activities had been at the centre of how our lives were organised in terms of what we did with our time and, to a large degree, who we spent time with. The church was our first port of call for support through the time Ben was ill. The church had prayed, visited and fed us throughout the year. They had been the people we turned to in our darkest hours.

As broken as we were, we still had an instinct to believe. As little as anything made sense at this point, we knew church and faith had been at the heart of making life work. We didn't get it, but we didn't feel like giving up.

Louise and I had both had a very real sense of having encountered God in different ways over a number of years. Louise remembers that, as a nine year old, a Methodist leader encouraged her to invite Jesus into her life. "Do it now, don't wait till you're older," he told her. That night she prayed in bed and felt the tingling of the Holy Spirit as God welcomed her into the family.

One time, when I was 21, I went away for three weeks on a mission called *Love Europe*. This started with a week's teaching and training. Full of angst, I took the opportunity to go and get some counselling. I sat down with two guys, one was American, one German. I expected to give them a potted version of my life history; my head was full of analysis about what had happened to me and what I needed from God. Pretty much as soon as the conversation had started the American guy turned to me and said, "You don't trust God because you've never trusted anyone." I was stunned into silence. I thought I knew myself, but this stranger had just summed up my life in a phrase. It was a major point in learning I needed to trust God, not get Him to rubber stamp my plans.

Our experience was of encounters with God that had changed us. God had enabled us to overcome the wounds and insecurities from our family's break ups. He had developed character in us so we could have a healthy marriage and be in a good place to bring up our children in a loving home.

So after Ben died we were in a place of spiritual shock, but we gravitated back to faith. We knew it had changed our lives and those of many people we'd known over the years.

A couple of weeks after Ben's celebration we went back to our faithful church, Living Waters Christian Fellowship. I'd been there 14 years and Louise and I had been there together for 11 years. It was 18 months since I'd taken on the leadership with Brian. During Ben's illness I hadn't been able to do much, though I preached the odd message when I had something I felt I could share. We'd missed most Sundays, church had come to us with constant visits and meals at home and the hospital.

I knew I was in no state to continue in leadership, but when we went back that Sunday we realised we couldn't handle it. The church was the same as usual, but we weren't the same people anymore. It was too much. We had to have painful conversations to tell people we were taking time out. We decided to go back to St Thomas' Crookes, the church we'd both come from years before, initially for 6 months to regroup.

St Tom's was a bigger church. A church where we could receive and recover, where we could start again. We could hide and talk to no one. We could go or not go, take part or not, and it didn't matter. We had the option to spectate, to consume. The worship was good, the teaching was good. If I didn't agree with a song, I didn't sing it. In truth I was a Christian, but not one who could really tell you much about what that meant.

I believed in God. I believed Jesus had died for my sins, but I wasn't praying, because that no longer seemed to make much sense, and I wasn't doing anything to pursue or develop my faith like reading the Bible. Spiritually we were shell-shocked.

We got back into the groove of going to church every week, just as we were used to. As we did that, we started to get to know people and got invited along to a barbecue hosted by a couple who led a midweek group. Soon we got into the rhythm of being a part of a small group again. These sessions generally involve eight to twelve people, with a bit of worship, Bible study and prayer and usually lots of cake. People were welcoming and, crucially, accepting of the fragility of our faith. Had people expected certainty of us we wouldn't have been able to cope. We were allowed to be ourselves, to share our struggles and confusion and begin to receive support with that.

One of the things the church tries to do is to get people involved so they are not a passive mass, expecting the leaders to do everything. One week Mick, the leader, said that if we wanted to be able to have communion and drinks at the end of the service people needed to volunteer to help, so Louise signed up for arranging communion and I signed up for tea making. In the small group people were asked to prepare different elements of the meeting, so we found ourselves uncomfortably preparing a bit of worship or leading the Bible questions. It felt weird, but it needed doing so we did what we could and were honest about how limited and weak we felt.

In this way we inched into deeper involvement. One Sunday Mick told us to pray for the person in front of us. He didn't give us a choice, so I did it and felt the familiar feeling of God guiding my prayers. At Christmas the church went into the town centre and gave out free mince pies as an expression of God's love. I didn't feel I could explain God to anyone, but I could give them a mince pie.

By Christmas we had decided to stay at St Tom's and the church titled its season of festive activities, "It's time to hope again". This was very powerful for us. We had survived the immediate aftermath of losing Ben, we had begun to re-group, and it began to feel that we could look forward and see hope for our future. As we reflected on that part of our spiritual journey, it felt that we hadn't ever lost faith, we had lost confidence. Slowly we were beginning to re-build that confidence. Fundamentally, we found out that whatever had happened and however we felt, God hadn't left.

What faith offered was the ability to do more than just survive. Keeping calm and carrying on is not a bad way to get by, but there has to be more to life than that.

By being in a church that expected God's Spirit to be at work in people's lives, and by being in community with others, we had a space to begin to be able to deal with our wounds. Both Louise and I had times in church where we lost it. Louise pretty much collapsed one day and was helped to a side room where people prayed until she recovered. Another time, I cried all over our friend Martin. In the small group people listened, accepting where we were and helping us to work through the fallout.

Grief can be like a magnet, drawing all sorts of other damaging emotions like anger, regret and guilt, which if they take hold, corrode life. We all face these emotions at some time. It's God Spirit who has had the power to prise these free.

Dealing with grief is hard and imprecise. It often feels like groping in the dark, not knowing if there is a destination to reach. Over time, some of the extreme reactions become clear. One is to get stuck in the past, frozen in time at the moment of loss. My dad told me a story of a colleague visiting a friend who'd lost a child in an accident years before. They showed them the child's room and nothing had been touched.

We were determined not to do that, not to be robbed of the future by living in the past. The other extreme is not to fixate on what's happened, but live in denial of it and act as if it hasn't happened. I've always found that if you push things under the carpet, you end up tripping over them.

Sometimes we worry that we have been too hard-headed and pragmatic in ploughing on. Do I push too many memories aside when they sting me? Have we grieved properly? But what does that even mean? How are you supposed to do this stuff?

Church was a place where we could wrestle and cry and shout, but people wouldn't just listen, they would pray, and as they prayed they would invite God to meet us, tend to our broken hearts and help us to deal with what would come next.

Church is not supposed to be a religious club. It's supposed to be a transformative community. It's frail and fallible, because of the people that make up the church, but in St Tom's we found a place of comfort and new hope. In time we ended up leading a small group ourselves and, after a few years, moved across town to live in Crookes, where the church is.

Of course, people ask the question, how we can still believe after all the prayers for Ben's healing failed? In short, faith makes more sense than anything else. Faith has been the thing that has helped us to move forward. As I move to look at the questions of faith this is a key point: questions of faith are questions about how we live. These were questions that I wrestled with. I didn't have the luxury of putting them off, because they were about knowing how we could face the future. So belief continued, but not as it had before.

Chapter Nine
Changing Belief – Facing the Questions

~~~

The day after Ben's last scan I took Joe down to Oxford for a treat that Louise had organised. We had been thinking about doing something special for Joe, who had had to put up with so much. Louise found out that his favourite author, Anthony Horowitz, was doing a series of book signings for the last book in his *Alex Rider* series. She was able to arrange for Joe to meet Anthony before the book signing and he very kindly gave Joe a special case full of merchandise.

On the train down, I had time to make sense of the news. Ben's cancer was rapidly advancing, our prayers had not stopped it. I didn't believe anymore that Ben was going to make it. As all of this spun round my head I got a mental picture that seemed to sum it all up: my worldview had been like a globe, which I was carrying round in a box. The globe looked impressive and helped me make sense of all that I saw and experienced. It felt solid and reliable. Then the bottom of the box broke, the globe shot through, and hit the ground. It didn't so much break as shatter. It was utterly destroyed; unsalvageable, unrecognisable, finished. I was left holding the box, shocked, bewildered. I was shattered.

I knew my worldview could never be the same again. My tidy faith was gone.

* * *

When your world is shattered as ours was, you are forced to question what you live by. I had believed in a God who could do anything. I had a theology that God would fix something as horrendous as we had faced. So in my own brokenhearted, meandering way, I had to confront the fact that I may have been following a myth. But I had a bigger and more immediate question: how could I live?

You see, the question of whether God is real is not an abstract matter of different ideas of truth to be calmly lined up and compared. We don't have the option of pausing life while we figure it all out. The issue was, and is, how am I going to keep going?

When I was nineteen I went to University with a confident faith, which I proceeded to share with people. In reality, I was sharing a set of recycled ideas, not personal knowledge of God. Pretty soon my ideas got shot down and I was left with a big crisis of faith. I remember spending the Christmas holidays wracked with doubt and being very clear about what it meant. I didn't see loss of faith as a release, I saw it as a void. I knew without God there was no hope and no

102

meaning. As someone without a comfortable home life or an obvious career path I could be defined by, I knew that there was no source of security and identity without my faith. So I wrestled and I fought and I found a faith I could build life upon – one that had credible historical roots and that was effective to straighten out my neuroses.

Make no mistake, I believe because I need to believe in God and if that makes me sound weak, I'm really not bothered.

So have there been times when I've doubted that God is there at all? Of course there have, and of course there still are. I'm not blind to the possibility that there may be no God and that those of us that believe in Him are just fooling ourselves. What I don't see is anyone suggesting anything better. What I don't see is any other hope to face the day.

Life is more fragile than we want it to be. The world around us would like to tell us that we can control life. We find this in self-help books, in advertising, in our children's education system. The truth is that we have *some* control, we have *lots of choices,* but the idea that we can control life is one of the biggest myths of our age. Life cannot be tamed. We do not sit at the helm of a control panel, we are more like surfers trying to stay afloat amidst the waves. We like the idea that we can box life – with technology, with plans, with performance management targets, with theologies that dictate to God – but none of it works. Life refuses to be contained by us.

Life often seems just too much doesn't it? I recently moved into a role in mental health to discover that the numbers suffering are huge and increasing, particularly amongst the young. In the words of another Athlete song, "the world is too heavy, too big for my shoulders. Come take the weight off me now." After Ben died, in the rawness and shock we needed help and we needed hope. We turned back to what we knew and it seemed that God was still around, most powerfully through the love of His people.

One of my early attempts to reconnect with God in the months after Ben's death was to put on a Christian CD. I found one by a band called *Delirious?* One of the songs jumped out at me. The words said that, "love will find a way to break through." That awakened something in me that God could do something, even in the place we were in, even after what we had been through. Something stirred in me to believe that this God that I was observing from a distance could be active in our lives again. A slow process of re-engagement began.

I believe that God is real and alive, whether I sense that at any given moment or not. When I doubted, in the months of distance from God, in all my confusion, He was, and is, still there. In our place of brokenness God's love was still at work, able to break through and bring healing and hope into our grief and cluelessness.

I believe because I need to believe. I need God. I can't prove He's there, but no one can disprove it, and unlike my teenage self, I'm not even slightly interested in having an argument about it. I believe because when I reach out to God, I find Him and find that, in fact, it was Him that was reaching out to me all along.

I had to go back to the basics of faith, which meant going back to Jesus. *The Message* translation of the Bible has a wonderful phrase that Jesus "took on flesh and moved into the neighbourhood". The Christian message that I was grappling with was of a God who chooses to get involved.

As the story goes, God turns up as a man. But not an all-conquering ruler, no, a helpless baby. Born in a backwater, into disgrace. Soon to become a refugee. The story continues that the man does nothing wrong. In time he becomes a leader. He teaches, He does miracles, He scandalises the religious authorities in favour of care for the outcasts over keeping the rules. So they eliminate the threat. They kill Him. Another crackpot dispatched. Only He won't stay dead. He rises again. He gathers His bedraggled followers and they form the church that spreads to every part of the globe.

He does what He said He'd do if they'd listened. He lays down His life, so that others can have life. He offers forgiveness and His Spirit to help us live this life.

The whole thing can be summed up in one word: *grace*. The story is that God steps in, reaches down, lifts us up. We don't have to do it ourselves, figure it out, fix it. Help is at hand. God's grace means God takes the initiative and keeps doing so.

Grace was the vicar coming for the music lesson. Grace was the youth ministry that gave me friends and hope. Grace was ending up in Sheffield, meeting Louise, homes, jobs and in all of that being changed from someone strangled by my past and my insecurities to someone who could learn to give, create, live a life that, in faltering ways, tries to make things better.

After Ben died, in the pain and confusion I found that that grace continued, through the love of the church, the offer of comfort for our broken hearts, the hope that good could still come.

The Christian faith comes down to this grace – the idea of a loving, creative God reaching out to His creation and showing the ultimate expression of how to step in. The passage below sums up this raw, passionate, selfless offer better than anything else I've read:

"Yeshua is a joke. He's less of a messiah, more something nasty on the pavement. And as he struggles on he recognises every roaring, jeering face. He knows our names. He knows our histories. And since, as well as being a weak and frightened man, he's also the love that makes the world, to whom all times and places are equally present, he isn't just feeling the anger and spite and unbearable self-disgust of this one crowd on this one Friday morning in Palestine; he's turning his bruised face towards the whole human crowd, past and present and to come, and accepting everything we have to throw at him, everything we fear we deserve ourselves. The doors of his heart are wedged open wide, and in rushes the pestilential flood, the vile and rolling tide of cruelties and failures and secrets. Let me take that from you, he is saying. Give that to me instead. Let me carry it. Let me be to blame instead. I am big enough. I am wide enough. I am not what you were told. I am not your king or your judge. I am the father who longs for every last one of his children. I am the friend who will never leave you. I am the light behind the darkness. I am the shining your shame cannot extinguish. I am the ghost of love in the torture chamber. I am change and hope. I am the refining fire. I am the door where you thought there was only wall. I am what comes after deserving. I am the earth that drinks the bloodstain. I am the gift without cost. I am. I am. I am. Before the foundation of the world I am.'[1]

Let me tell you what I think I know.

I think that a world that talks about God as an out of date myth has nothing to replace Him with. The world is full of lovely people, but is defined by insecurity, cynicism and disappointment. Beyond the bling, the hype and the clever computers that rule us, but are always bloody crashing, we live in a world full of poverty, banality and emptiness.[2]

I think this guy Jesus that walked the earth 2000 years ago offers something that is unmatched by any other movement or individual in history – a vision of a better life and the help to get there.

I think that for all my anguish and bewilderment at losing Ben, when all is said and done God is still there. He is not the God I want Him to be, He just is.

* * *

Crookes where we live now is at the top of one of Sheffield's big hills. From our kitchen window we can see a big sky, always with a different cloudscape, and each morning as I blearily make a cup of tea, I see the sun peeking through and at times I remember my pre-scan prayer to the big God of the clouds.

The whole point of God is that He's supposed to be big. That's why most people pray at some time. When we're up against it, we want a Superman moment from God. When that doesn't happen some give up on the idea of God, while others are left in a place of angry accusation. You would be mad not to question: is there a God and if so what's the point of Him? Seriously, how could we still believe in this God who has failed us?

The key question for me has become: what sort of God do I believe in? And following that, what does it mean to believe in Him? I'm taken back to that much quoted verse from Jeremiah:

"'For I know the plans I have for you,' declares the Lord, 'plans to prosper you and not to harm you, plans to give you hope and a future.'" (Jeremiah 29:11)

Christians can take verses like this to mean that God has a detailed secret blueprint for our lives. We can end up thinking our job is to find out what the plan is, so we can run with it. I remember as a young man lots of Christians who were seeking a "word for their lives" so they could get on with doing what God had called them to do. This can lead to angst about how to correctly discern what God is saying and the fear of getting it wrong and straying from the path that God has marked out. Beneath it all we can interpret the verse to say that, in the end, God has a plan for everything to work out.

The problem is that things like losing your kid don't seem to fit into that idea very well. Surely that couldn't be in the plan? So what does it mean to believe God has plans for our lives?

In 2013, two years after losing Ben, I was told that my great job with the Council was going to be deleted. In the summer, I was that told there were a number of jobs I could apply for, to be redeployed, but there were no guarantees. In my uncertainty I prayed and I believe God spoke. By spoke, I mean ideas came into my mind in a way I've come to recognise over the years as being from God.

As I prayed, I asked God what was going to happen and He said, "I will be with you." I was not that impressed! I wanted a clear answer, I wanted guidance. If I had magicked up reassurance from within myself I would have expected something better than that. The impression was clear: God wasn't going to give me the straight answer I wanted, He wanted me to trust Him. I knew that depending on how I reacted, the news that God would be with me was either the best or worst news going. For someone clamouring for clarity this was not good. But beyond that, God was telling me that He would be there. I would not be alone. I would not be abandoned.

Months later, with redundancy weeks away, I had my fifth job interview of the year. I was well prepared, but feeling the stress. I was sure that this was my last shot at getting a good job with the Council. I wrestled with the uncertainty of not knowing what was ahead. On the day of the interview a friend texted me a Bible verse: *"Be still and know that I am God"* (Psalm 46:10). This was what I needed to hear; this was God speaking. I couldn't know what would happen at the interview, but I could know that God was with me.

I got the job. God had provided again. Just like the time when Louise and I were due to marry and, in the few months ahead, we needed to buy a house and needed a job for Louise in Sheffield. We got both. Just like the time I was working for the church and was told to get a job in the real world and I needed one by the beginning of the next year. I got one. I know what you're thinking. If God can intervene with jobs and houses, why couldn't he intervene with Ben? I know and I don't know, but the message was clear: He was with us.

I have had to learn to think about the idea of God's plans in a different way, because tragedy doesn't fit well with the idea that's it all going to be a march of victory till we get to glory.

The story of Christmas is known as the incarnation – the idea that God came to be with us as a baby, born into a mucky stable to live, initially, a very ordinary life. This tells us something important about the nature of God, which is that He is prepared to get stuck in, to get involved in normal life.

So what were God's plans for Ben? The message of encouragement that he wouldn't die was wrong. It had to be. We all die. We all face struggles. Any plan of God has to deal with that or it's just our delusions. The plan we need from God is a plan of how to live in a world that includes fear, suffering and uncertainty. That is the world we know we all inhabit.

It would have been fantastic for Ben to live a long life, to be happy and productive. Ideally to captain West Ham to a Champions League win before bringing world peace as the head of the United Nations.

But what if the plan was different? What if the plan was that Ben, in whatever life he lived, knew love – most of all the love of the God who'd made him?

What if the plan is to know God and to live a life that blesses others and shows His goodness? If that's the plan, then the plan was fulfilled.

What if the plan is not principally pleasure, longevity and material gain, but living the God-life by entering what Jesus called the Kingdom of heaven, where faith is not about church attendance or a set of rules, but living under the shadow of our Creator to live a life of peace, hope and generosity?

From this perspective, the plan of God is to inhabit our lives. It's not a path to a shiny, final destination where all the loose ends are tied up, but a life lived hand in hand with our loving Father.

* * *

After Ben died, my theology – my understanding of God – was essentially broken. My faith hadn't disappeared, but initially it lay dormant because I didn't get how to function as a Christian anymore. Over time I have pieced things together again and ended up with a faith that is more real and able to handle uncertainty.

All I can tell you is where I've got to. This means talking about suffering and about what prayer is supposed to be able to do about that. In some ways, all my questions come back to one: *how could God let Ben get ill and die?*

The question is stupefying. How could it happen and how could a God of love and power allow it? There are times, after having years to get used to Ben not being here, when I can consider this in a measured, vaguely logical way. Other times, as I said before, the fact of it is like being punched in the head. That's the problem. This isn't a question of philosophy, but of pain.

Pain is a part of our world. "Life is hard," one of my A-level lecturers once told my class, "get used to it." We can't escape pain. The big thing is what is there to help us.

But that's not to cop out in terms of why the problem is there in the first place. Why did Ben have to get ill?

I don't believe God gives people cancer, but if I believe in a God who can heal then I have to accept that in this case He chose not to, especially when confronted with the fact that He chose to step in miraculously in intensive care. In some way God allowed this and God allows a world in which horrible stuff happens.

I remember a conversation with Joe where I told him that, at times, I struggled with why Ben had died. "Cancer" was his blunt reply. Why did Ben die? Because he got ill. I believe he got ill and God took him home.

This isn't a time to start banging on about free will and Adam and Eve and the Fall. We know that humans are to blame for a lot of the world's suffering, but not something like a gorgeous 5-year old getting cancer. More helpful, for me at least, is not these type of circular debates, but to question what our expectation of life and our kid's lives is. We assume we will all live long, healthy lives, but that's not been the case historically and is still not the case in plenty of parts of the world. We are fortunate to live in a rich, advanced country. We think we have a right to live long and prosper, and if there is a God that should be His priority. We seek a God of happy circumstances or dismiss the idea of one that can't offer that.

What's helpful for me is to have an eternal perspective. Unsurprisingly, for the father who's lost his boy, I want to believe in heaven and I do. I believe Ben got ill and God took him home. I remember the picture the visiting speaker had of God's hand reaching down. We wrestled with God for Ben to be healed until we had to accept that he wouldn't be. The best for Ben would clearly have been for him to never get ill, but after all that he had been through, what would have been left had Ben survived? The sight loss, memory loss, breathing problems, stomach problems, more than anything the risk of the cancer coming back... We so yearned to keep Ben, but now we believe he is fully restored and rocking and rolling in heaven. I feel closest to Ben when I worship God in church, because I think that's what he is doing too.

I still believe in the God who makes sense of life, who shows me a way to keep going and move forward. I believe, but not in the way that I once did. The globe shattered.

The simplest expression of my new theology is that I no longer believe that because I am a Christian I can know what will happen. Nowadays I believe that because I am a Christian I can know that God will be with me, whatever happens.

I believe in a God who steps into the mess, but I don't believe He stops life being messy. My expectations of God have changed. More practically, so have my expectations of praying to Him.

As I started to reconnect with God, I had to start to tackle questions about prayer, something that had gone from being a constant pursuit when Ben was ill to non-existent after he died. I didn't know where to start; I didn't get it. I needed to deal with the questions: does prayer work? And linked to that, can you believe in prophecies? We prayed and prayed and central to that was the belief that God was speaking to people as we prayed. Didn't God say Ben wouldn't die? Didn't God give us the snow prophecy? Didn't He say we would take everything back?

Well did He?

We were sat at the table one day doing Maths homework. Louise got a text. Her colleague's recently born baby was sick. What did we do? We prayed. It's what we do – we bring things to God.

Does prayer work and, more to the point, is God arbitrary? Why does He sometimes seem to get involved and other times stand back? You know, of course, that I can't answer, not really. I do believe God hears our prayers and sometimes He agrees with what we ask for. Sometimes, we see later that what we asked for wasn't the best plan and sometimes we just don't get it.

I do believe God speaks. Sometimes it all matches up nicely – God speaks and unlocks a situation, prayers drive other prayers and things change. In intensive care it felt like that. Sometimes we hear what we want to hear, not the voice of God, but over time we get more discerning and also accepting of our limits. People are fallible so prophecy is too, but in community with wise people, light gets shed.

I do believe in miracles. I think the world is extraordinary and miraculous. I don't buy that it's a fluke or a closed system, but I don't believe we can order up miracles and these days I would run a mile from anyone who said they could.

The best gauge for this as a Christian is the Bible and it is very helpful to look at the life of the first Christians in the early church. Here was a group of people, transformed from a cowering, defeated rabble to a society-changing movement by the resurrection and visitations of Jesus. They were then dramatically filled with the power of His Spirit and started doing extraordinary things, like seeing people healed in the name of Jesus. Following the teaching of Jesus and the example of these church founders, I still believe it is right to pray for healing. I know it can happen and I want to see it happen, but does the early church demonstrate the idea of fully restored dominion?

In Acts chapter 7, Stephen was stoned to death for his faith. Not a great result. Certainly not an earthly victory. Couldn't he have slipped away like Jesus when the crowd threatened to stone him? It would seem not.

What about Paul, the pillar of the early church, miraculously transformed from a murderer of Christians to an all-out promoter of their faith? Paul was beaten up a number of times, shipwrecked, imprisoned.

Most of the founding fathers of the church paid with their lives. God was a reality to them. God used them to do astounding things, change lives, build transformational worshipping communities which reached the ends of the earth. What they weren't able to do was just pray all the bad stuff away. I don't believe that is what God promises. God's job is not to make all our dreams come true like a Disney film. I believe God offers His presence to enrich our lives and those of the people around us, not because He gives us a silver bullet in prayer, but because He offers to be with us come what may.

The problem with the idea that Christians can recover some perfect state of dominion is that it pretends we can spiritually overcome our failures and frailties to get to some kind of advanced spiritual state. I believe that the more I draw near to God, the more He draws near to me and I can know Him more and my life will work better. However, I don't believe there is some kind of higher level to attain where I spiritually click my fingers and all the bad stuff flees.

The alarming place that this kind of theology leads to is the idea for Christians that our lives are dependent on how good or bad we are at being Christians. We take the mastery away from God and pretend we can take the mystery out of life. After Ben died, the question was asked: *what did we miss in our prayers?* Literally, how did we fall short in our ability to pray, in the thousands of hours of others' prayers, with rooms full of church leaders and visits to healing ministries – what did we fail to discern and pray to get Ben healed? It's hard for parents of kids who get cancer not to wrack their brains to think if there was something, anything, they could have done, to in some way be responsible for their child getting cancer without adding being spiritually deficient to the list. Ben didn't die because of how we brought him up. Ben didn't die because we didn't get the right medical help sooner. Ben didn't die because we got our prayers wrong. Ben got ill and God chose to take him home.

Good theology makes sense of what we're like and shows what can be done about it. Christianity is about recognising our need for God. It's about accepting His grace in reaching out to us and choosing to follow Him. It's about laying down pride. It's not about getting God to do what we want.

So yes, I believe, but my idea of God and faith has changed.

I don't believe you can rustle up a miracle. A miracle is just that – a miracle. I believe they happen and we got one that prolonged Ben's life and helped us to deal with his death, but miracles are not ordinary and every day.

I reject the idea of a performance-based faith. As someone involved in leading a group in church, I will continue to encourage people to seek more of God, but we are encouraging people to access His boundless grace, not to become good at being Christians. That really isn't the point. God is God, not us. Being a Christian is about inviting Him to take charge and lead the way.

How does prayer work? I don't believe you can turn prayer into a formula to get God to answer. Prayer is communication with God. Prayer is about relationship. I wish, when Ben was ill, I had spent a bit more time just being with God, not barking spiritual orders at Ben's sickness.

Christians talk about life as a spiritual battle and about spiritual warfare – the idea that in God's name we are taking on the work of the devil. This can easily lead to spiritual pride and the idea that we can take on the bad guy. You end up looking for spiritual keys, that higher level, but in reality the Christian faith is supposed to be pretty simple – relationship with the God who made us and is there for us. Just as miracles are miracles, not typical occurrences, prayer is just prayer – it's talking to God.

Why did we get one miracle and not another? Because I think that's what God decided. He chose to take Ben home and whilst that was the worst thing imaginable for us, it wasn't for him. The exuberant boy with the simple faith is partying with his Maker.

Underneath our questions is pain. Fundamentally we ask, how come bad things happen? Yet the world as we know it does contain pain and suffering, and more than anything we need to know how to face that. In reality, suffering shocks us. It wounds, it numbs. We recoil, breathless, flailing for some sense in it.

Here's the thing for me about suffering – more important than the sheer horror of it – something needs to be done about suffering. And whilst we can rage against it, we need someone to step in. And God does. He steps in to help and sustain. He provides. He comforts.

The Christian story is of God as man stepping in, taking the pain and making a way out of it. God gets suffering. He has suffered for us.

We can choose to reject God because He doesn't match up to our expectations. As I've prayed more recently about house moves and jobs I've had to accept that God, while bothered (and subsequently showing He could provide) is not the God of making my circumstances happy.

The answer for me is not a tidy answer or a tidy faith. The answer, frustratingly, is to let God be God, not the way I want Him to be.

God is not Clark Kent waiting for our emergency so that he can burst out as Superman. God is the creating and sustaining force behind life. He offers a new way of doing things, where His values change us and, through that, change the world around us. Jesus and the early church show that this Kingdom often confounds our expectations. God is not a supernatural turbo boost to allow us to master the materialistic, control freak society we live in. Jesus offers strength for the weak, laying down His life so we can start again, and inviting us to use our lives to make things better.

The point of God, annoyingly, is not to do our bidding. The point of God is that He offers to walk the journey with us.

Endnotes

1. Francis Spufford, *Unapologetic*

2. "The people of the modern West are better fed, better housed, better equipped with health care than those in any previous age in human history. But, paradoxically, they also seem to be the most fearful, the most lonely, the most superstitious, and the most bored generation in human history. All the labour saving devices of modern technology have only enhanced human stress, and modern life is characterised by a restless movement from place to place, from one 'experience' to another, in a frenetic whirl of purposeless activity." (Vinoth Ramachandra, *Gods That Fail*).

Chapter Ten
The New Normal

~~

Work became a very difficult place for Louise this year. The situation left her questioning her ability to teach and whether she had the strength to keep going. I felt like she could go under at any point. I knew that we had to get people praying in an organised way, not just as a one off request. Louise set up a WhatsApp group where she could ask for prayer for specific needs and issues. In response, people prayed and posted prayers, Bible verses and words of encouragement. There was no overnight fix, but Louise was lifted and strengthened and was able to carry on. The tide began to turn and God made a way out. Louise is back working in the village where we used to live, where we have friends, and where Ben is buried. Louise feels that God has brought her home.

* * *

So much has changed since we lost Ben. We've moved

house. We've moved church. Joe has changed school. We've both changed jobs a few times. We didn't have the option of things staying the same. Some of these changes would have happened if Ben hadn't got ill – life doesn't stand still – but fundamentally we have had to find a new life and establish a new normal.

As we faced losing Ben and dealt with its aftermath, we had to find positive things to cling to. We had to do what we could with what we had. As we did this, we realised that was the spirit Ben had epitomised. Ben ran his race. He ran as far and as hard as he could, and his life has profoundly touched the lives of dozens of people he met. Now, we have to run our race as well as we can.

A guy called Ron Dunn wrote a book called *When Heaven Is Silent*. In it he says that the question, "Why me?" is the wrong question. That may sound crass and unfeeling, but Ron Dunn lost his son too, so he has the right to talk about this stuff. "Why me?" is the wrong question because though utterly understandable, it cannot be answered and can only lead to despair. The right question, Ron says, is "What do I do next?" That's where you find the future.

You don't always get what you want. Your dreams don't always come true. Authentic faith cannot pretend that we get to make God be the God we want.

* * *

God walks with us even where the ground is more bumpy than we'd like. In Psalm 23 God makes it clear that He will be our guide on the road. He doesn't promise that He will make everything okay, but He promises we will never be left alone:

> *"The* LORD *is my shepherd, I shall not be in want. He makes me lie down in green pastures, he leads me beside quiet waters, he restores my soul. He guides me in paths of righteousness for his names sake. Even though I walk through the darkest valley of the shadow of death, I will fear no evil, for you are with me; your rod and your staff, they comfort me. You prepare a table before me in the presence of my enemies. You anoint my head with oil; my cup overflows. Surely your goodness and love will follow me all the days of my life, and I will dwell in the house of the* LORD *forever."* (Psalm 23)

What does faith look like now? This new, more real, less tidy faith? It's not a downgraded faith. It's not that we expect less from God, but we presume less and we pretend less that we have our head around it all.

Faith is a journey with God as our companion. It's not about having it all together, it's about being able to do something about the fact that we haven't got it all together. Faith means we share the journey with precious friends in a praying community. We have the privilege of being able to bare our souls with friends and help carry each other's loads.

In the Bible Jesus uses the picture of an ox with a yoke on

its back to pull a plough to say that His "yoke is easy" and his "burden is light". He offers to help, to shape things, so we are not weighed down, so that life can fit better. The yoke He offers is not all about what I can or cannot do, but what He can help me to do through His grace. In reality, I switch between both, but there is help and hope on hand. There is an alternative to the burn out or cynicism we see all around us.

I do not float around my office in a bubble of bliss. At times, I worry and swear and slag people off with the best of them, but I know that having done that, there is a better way possible; that next time can be different.

God has helped me to forgive people I've hated. God has helped me like people I couldn't stand. God broke into my teenage insecurity and arrogance and started fixing me. He did the same for Louise and stopped us repeating the cycle of broken relationships we'd come from. God has brought us into the path of many wonderful people, people without whom we wouldn't have coped during Ben's illness and after his death. In this and many more mundane times God has shown me what to do when I'm stuck.

God has shown us that there is still much to live for, good things are on the horizon, life is still full of opportunity, ideas can flow again. This is the God I know – a creative God who wants me to live a creative, productive life. Grace rescues and then becomes a springboard to a better life.

Grace means that when it's all too much, when I'm at the end of myself, there is a release of the pressure valve of trying to get it all right, all the time. I do not have to pretend that I am in perfect control or that I ever will be.

Let me tell what our belief isn't.

Belief isn't pretending everything's okay. I'm not saying I never say "fine" when I'm asked how I am, but I certainly didn't say I was fine in the months after Ben had died. We told people straight just how we felt. To their credit no one at St Tom's struggled with that. Our faith is not some kind of denial-based, faith expression of the "positive mental attitude" that people peddle to tell you that if you try hard enough everything will feel okay.

Belief is having someone to go to about the fact that things aren't okay. This book is not about saying that we have come out the other side and everything is fine now. Life without Ben is hard. On the whole, we have been able to adapt. I can only attribute that to the prayer we have been deluged with, as I have lost count of the number of bereaved parents who say that time is not a healer. We have learned pretty well how to live without Ben. We have a life full of good things. We don't live in a state of mourning, but grief can resurface at any time. The fabric of life will tear and all of the pain of Ben's death will march in like it happened yesterday. Anything can trigger this, because Ben is everywhere, he is a part of us. We don't just remember him, we can still picture him and imagine how he would be if he was with us, what he would think of what we're doing or eating or laughing at.

Without Ben we are misshapen, incomplete; life is not

how it should be, all that it could be. We are busy and active, we don't try and block Ben out, but at times the gaps in life feel like they are yawning and we just have to try and work around them. We miss him. We will always have an element of loneliness without him.

Ben's death shocks me as much as ever. At times I will tell someone about him or see a photo I've not seen for a while or stand at his grave and just not be able to take it in. My boy, my beautiful boy. How can it be?

A while back I found Ben's dedication certificate. Rather than having him baptised, we gave thanks to God for him and offered his life back up to God. What was that about I wondered? What good did that do? But what did I expect? That I could demand that God would give him the life I ordered? I don't think that's the point anymore – to prescribe to Him. I'm learning that the point is that He is for us and with us, whatever comes.

What is our story? The story I've spent the past couple of years trying and failing to tell properly? The story is that life as bereaved parents can be good again. We are not just surviving, we are more than surviving. Alongside the pain there is blessing and joy. There is hope. That hope is that we do not walk this road alone and that we will see Ben again one day and worship our God together.

God is there to sustain, support and shape. In the pain and

the frustration God steps in, just as Jesus did 2000 years ago. God is with us. We are not alone. Despite the heartache and pain we can look back and say that God has been faithful.

For me the bottom line is this: when all is quiet and still, when all the busyness stops, what is left is me and God. And as I embrace God, everything shifts into place. I steady like the bubble in a spirit level, I find my peace, my refuge, my guide. Everything else in this frenetic world can be seen for what it is – so much froth and bluster. All that is man-made, short-term and shallow fades in the presence of the One who made it all. And there is nothing better.

> *Yes, I'll sing the wondrous story*
> *Of the Christ Who died for me,*
> *Sing it with the saints in glory,*
> *Gathered by the crystal sea.*
> (I will sing the wondrous story by Francis Rowley)

Ben Luck.
September 22nd 2004 to eternity.
Keeping Jesus busy.

Thanks

~~~

One of the purposes of this book was to give thanks to the many people that helped us during Ben's illness and after his death.

Thank you to the friends, family and church family that held us together and kept us going.

Thank you to all the staff at the Children's Hospital, Weston Park Hospital and Bluebell Wood Hospice who cared for us all with such unstinting professionalism, dedication and humanity.

Thank you to everyone who prayed. Without being able to explain how I can tell you with confidence that none of that was wasted. Particular thanks to the legendary Al, Martin, Giles and Ray; the wonderful folk at Living Waters Christian Fellowship and the children, families and staff of St Josephs School.

Many people have read different versions of the book and given their honest feedback – sorry to any I forget, but huge thanks to Rebecca, Colin, Jamie, Casey, Carl, Mick, Alan, Tom, Pete, Paula, Giles, Lindsey, Mags, Joy, Mum, Dad and my treasured Louise and Joe.

Thanks to Tim at River Publishing for believing in this book and guiding me through the process.

The greatest thanks of all to God for all He has given me, for His boundless grace, His unwavering faithfulness and unending hope.